MW01165050

Copyright 2006

Published by
Integritous Press
PO Box 5043
Phillipsburg, NJ
08865

Library of Congress Cataloging-in-Publication Data

Fantina, Steven P.
Of Thee I Speak/Steven Fantina 1st ed.
ISBN 10--0-9745669-1-8
First Printing 2006

Printed in the United States of America

It is safe to say that this book never would have been written had September 11, 2001 remained an anonymous date in history. Alas, that day of incomprehensible evil did take place and--cliché or not--changed everything!

For a number of years I have been webmaster/editor of Word of the Day (www.wordofthedaywebsite.com) emailing a daily vocabulary builder to thousands of subscribers. A few days after September 11, I--like everyone else in the civilized world--was trying to carry on and got the idea to add an inspiring, patriotic quote to that day's word. I typed in "force is all-conquering, but its victories are short-lived.--Abraham Lincoln" and emailed it along with the Word of the Day (WOTD.) The next day I tacked on another relevant aphorism to the daily word; this time choosing "the law...dictated by God himself is, of course, superior in obligation to any other. It is binding over all the globe, in all countries, and at all times. No human laws are of any validity if contrary to this. --Alexander Hamilton"

The inclusion of these pertinent sayings seemed to work so I kept it up, never giving any thought to how long this temporary feature would remain a part of WOTD, but had I contemplated the matter I would have predicted its addition to be ephemeral. But the patriotic segment endured, and I started collecting felicitous quotations and kept them in a separate email file.

About a year and a half later I inadvertently sent out the file of pending quotes instead of the WOTD. My embarrassment over such an obvious blunder quickly abated when the feedback started to arrive in my inbox. The mistaken submission elicited more responses than WOTD had ever previously generated, and every single message was positive. Months later I received requests to send the quotes again! Now over four years since the first major strike in the War on Terror was fired upon the American homeland, the patriotic quotes remain not only a fixture of Word of the Day but are unquestionably its most popular element--far surpassing the allure of the words.

Since the Words involved in WOTD made their way into a book (the interminably titled *101 Words You'll Probably Never Need To Know But Can Use To Impress People*), its most captivating components seemed to warrant a tome as well. Thus, *Of Thee I Speak* was born.

Prior to the terrorist attacks, a book like this may not have made it into print, but there was a large clandestine market for it. Latent patriotism stirred deep inside most of us, but we had given into the politically correct dictates that told us to stifle it. In some ways we owe al-Qaeda a debt of gratitude for breaking the dam and letting our natural love for America gush out freely. There is nothing wrong with admitting or even bragging about living in the greatest nation on earth.

While this work acknowledges the obvious reality that the United States is far superior to every other country, in no way is it trying to say that America is without its flaws. The legacy of slavery will forever tarnish our history. The Trail of Tears and Japanese internment camps never should have happened. More recently we were shocked to see federal authorities--without provocation--slaughter eighty-seven men, women, and children in the Branch Davidian compound just outside of Waco, and in the tragic Elian Gonzales case, we witnessed the highest levels of our federal government unleash 150 machine gun-wielding thugs to kidnap a six-year-old child away from his loving family and return him to a life of slavery in Cuba. These inexcusable atrocities can never be brushed aside or mitigated in their heinousness. Still, these gross infringements are vile exceptions in a long, proud, honorable history. In many other nations, such breaches are mundane occurrences. The United States of America is the envy of the world because it is free and allows all a chance to prosper. It is the many good elements of America that *Of Thee I Speak* boldly salutes.

Some may ponder how I selected the thirteen categories for this work. Actually, the quotes determined the classifications themselves. The bulk of these entries are quotes that I had already gathered, and as I tried to organize them appropriately, the categories easily fell into place. The chapters included here in no way present an exhaustive list. Entire sections could have been devoted to Exploration, Inventions, Landmarks, American Firsts, the American Family, American Holidays, etc. Indeed each topic could fill a volume like this several times over. Similarly, the quotations chosen here comprise only a tiny fraction of the lines appropriate to a work of this nature.

The chapter devoted to the Military does not do justice to all American wars. Even the briefest battle could produce a booklet thicker than this. The eloquent statements of many notable Americans did not make it into this edition because no book of this nature could be anywhere near conclusive.

As to the sayings that made it into print, there were no complex criteria used in the selection process. Commonly known quotes--regardless of their power--do not appear in these pages. The profundity of Abraham Lincoln's "a house divided against itself cannot stand," Franklin Delano Roosevelt's "we have nothing to fear but fear itself," or Martin Luther King Jr.'s "I have a dream that my four little children will one day live in a nation where they will not be judged by the color of their skin but by the content of their character" is certainly no less plangent than the chosen phrases, but their familiarity to most Americans would render their placement here superfluous. While many of the quotes are relevant to more than one category, each appears where it appeared to fit most suitably.

Regarding how the book is arranged, each section offers a brief introductory synopsis then several pages of quotes from a salmagundi of speakers. The words of Americans (the vast majority of included citations) are written in standard print. The few contributions of non-Americans are printed in a noticeably different font. In the Iraqi Liberation and September 11 chapters some of the most appropriate lines were spoken long before the described events transpired. Quotes of this nature are written in italicized print. Following each collection of shorter quotes is a reprinted, essay or speech that deftly examines a related subject in more detail. These pieces from an assortment of voices--some well known, some not--are elegantly written, cogently convey the author's or speaker's message, and will leave the reader feeling even better about being an American.

Finally, as to how the quotes were chosen. First and foremost with the exception of the Immigration chapter where minimal steps were taken to obtain the words of immigrants from many countries, absolutely no effort was made to achieve a diverse or multicultural cross section of Americans. (That may be very hard to believe considering the aggregate authors of the longer pieces; yet by aiming to get the best of the Great Melting Pot sometimes you will find people of different backgrounds and sometimes you won't.) The criteria used to warrant inclusion was merely that the speaker adroitly express a sincere patriotic sentiment. Words of the Founding Fathers and celebrated Americans from history appear alongside the ideas of many ordinary Americans whose names will be known by few outside their families. The selected phrases come from recent immigrants and Americans who trace their ancestry back to the *Mayflower*. They come from famous names in the fields of sports, science, entertainment, literature, and politics. Nearly every president is spotlighted a few times, and some foreign friends and admirers are sprinkled in the mix too. In the September 11 and Iraq chapters the too-often stifled voices of patriotic Muslim citizens are generously featured.

So while this work is certainly not all-encompassing, it puts forth a respectful blending of the words and phrases that have made America great--sung by an arrayed chorus of Americans whose actions on behalf of their country have spoken louder than even these ornate words ever could.

For Michael and Mary Fantina, two true patriots--the son of Italian immigrants and an immigrant from Newfoundland (now part of Canada) --who married in 1945 and raised an American family whose youngest child edited this book. After sixty years of marriage they still appreciate and demonstrate what is best about America and instilled the same patriotism in their children and grandchildren.

Generally when someone puts out a book, it is his or her own words that make or break it, but with *Of Thee I Speak* it is the words of many others that provide its heart and soul.

To all those great Americans (and a few loyal friends) who have gone before and those still striving to make the country even better, thanks for the sayings that form the backbone of this book. I am convinced that the reprinted complete works included in this work are truly magical, and special thanks go to Eric L. Strickland, Eugene Chin Yu, David Yeagley, Adam Cirucci, Mike North, and Peter Schramm for allowing me to use their scintillating commentaries. Along with the contributions of President George W. Bush, Former Interim-Iraqi Prime Minister Ayad Alawi, Pope John Paul II, National Endowment for the Humanities Chairman Bruce Cole, and Secretary Elihu Root, these treatises add so much vibrancy to this work. Thanks also to those at the White House Counsel's Office who patiently explained the process of reprinting President Bush's speeches and to Erik Lokkesmoe at NEH for clarifying the steps to reuse Chairman Cole's words.

Deep gratitude goes to Hazel Mitchell for composing the captivating cover picture that so enchantingly embodies the essence of this work and to Adam Sommers for his meticulous proofreading.

Finally, thanks go to Todd Denys, Esquire for his guidance in ensuring that all necessary measures were employed to see that this book was published in accordance with the principles of the Fairness Doctrine.

Every reasonable effort was made to determine the exact accuracy of each quote, but in certain cases where primary sources are no longer available, secondary sources had to suffice.

Table of Contents

MILITARY

It is foolish and wrong to mourn the men who died. Rather we should thank God that such men lived.-- George S. Patton

It was hard to put the rest of the book in order because the topics covered in chapters 2--13 are all vitally important, so the remaining sections are placed randomly. However the first chapter had to pay tribute to the book's most vital subject--the American Military. As all American citizens and everyone else with an iota of common sense know, without the American military--there is no freedom, no justice, no elections, no America! No other organization has ever fostered as much good worldwide as the United States' military.

The patriots who fought in the Revolutionary War gave birth to the Land of the Free and established the world's beacon of liberty. Black and White soldiers fought with honor on both sides of the Civil War, and righted our gravest internal wrong. In both World Wars America's military was called upon to rid the world of evil forces of fascism and bravely met its challenges. Wars in Korea and Vietnam were hindered by political intrusiveness, and our military was withdrawn before its missions had been accomplished. Both locations remain smoldering outposts of unease decades after bureaucratic interference prevented assured military victories. Yet American servicemen demonstrated great valor in both conflicts despite the partisan meddling. Soldiers, Sailors, Airmen, Marines, and Coast Guard personnel stood our ground throughout the Cold War's deep freeze. Today the American military is leading the worldwide fight against the borderless enemy of terror. In between these major clashes lesser skirmishes from Tripoli in the early 1800s to Grenada in 1983 have called our military to act quickly, resolutely, and tirelessly. Every single time the answer has been the same. American warriors have displayed unequivocal courage and outstanding soldiering in meeting duty's exigent demands.

America's affinity for those who protect us is powerful and unwavering. Even people who know no one currently serving feel a potent kinship with the troops, and the innate bond only intensifies whenever American servicemen are called into harm's way. The esteem for our troops is not even limited to Americans. Our fighting forces are respected around the world--feared by those who wish us harm and revered by those who seek their aid or protection. Grateful Europeans celebrated when American forces liberated Hitler's concentration camps. Contrary to popular revisionism, the Vietnamese people cried when American forces were withdrawn, and many of them made their way to our shores after Communism overran their homeland. Today we see fifty million liberated Iraqis and Afghanis venerating our troops who are helping rid their own countries of heartless killers. Many others throughout the Middle East and other oppressed states long for the sight of Americans in uniform to signal their own emancipation.

To those who have served in the military no expression of thanks is sufficient from those of us who enjoy freedom's bounty, but strangely enough none ever seems necessary because fulfilling humanity's highest calling provides its own reward.

Unfortunately the quotes in the section are not evenly divided among all American conflicts. Some wars are only given scant mention, but the sentiments expressed are timeless and salute all who have ever nobly donned the American uniform.

Let us recollect that peace or war will not always be left to our option; that however moderate or unambitious we may be, we cannot count upon the moderation or hope to extinguish the ambition of others.--Alexander Hamilton

To be prepared for war is one of the most effectual means of preserving peace.--George Washington

Only a peace between equals can last.--Woodrow Wilson

The patriot volunteer, fighting for country and his rights, makes the most reliable soldier on earth.--Thomas J. Jackson

The nation that forgets its defenders will itself be forgotten. --Calvin Coolidge

Over the years, the United States has sent many of its fine young men and women into great peril to fight for freedom beyond our borders. The only amount of land we have ever asked for in (consequence) is enough to bury those who did not return. --Colin Powell

Neither I, nor any man I served with, ever committed any atrocity or war crime in Vietnam. The opposite was the truth. Rather than use excessive force, we suffered casualty after casualty because we chose to refrain from firing rather than risk injuring civilians. More than once, I saw friends die in areas we entered with loudspeakers rather than guns.--John O'Neil[1]

I do not believe that war and military service are the only means to honor in America. God grants us all the privilege of having our character and our patriotism tested. But those who wear the uniform of the United States know better than anyone the meaning of American citizenship.--John McCain

A young man who does not have what it takes to perform military service is not likely to have what it takes to make a living.--John F. Kennedy

A hero is no braver than an ordinary man, but he is braver five minutes longer.--Ralph Waldo Emerson

These men came here to storm these beaches for one purpose only, not to gain anything for ourselves, not to fulfill any ambitions that America had for conquest, but just to preserve freedom...Many thousands of men have died for such ideals as these...but these young boys were cut off in their prime. --Dwight D. Eisenhower on D-Day

There is immoral violence and there is moral violence. --Dennis Prager[2]

One man with courage makes a majority.--Andrew Jackson

There is a price which is too great to pay for peace, and that price can be put in one word. One cannot pay the price of self-respect. --Woodrow Wilson

I'm not expecting any more than a few restless hours of sleep snatched upright in a rough truck seat, but even that suddenly seems a great luxury. For no sleep at all and conceivably not even another sweet day of life--would accrue to me or the other(s)...if it wasn't for a handful of tough men willing to force themselves awake all night...They are literally the only reason that I (and at a longer range, you and the rest of America) can drift off peacefully when slumber beckons.--Karl Zinsmeister, embedded in Iraq[3]

When we assumed the Soldier, we did not lay aside the Citizen. --George Washington

The harder the conflict, the more glorious the triumph.
--Thomas Paine

It's the soldier not the reporter who gives you the freedom of the press. It's the soldier not the poet who gives you the freedom of speech. It's the soldier not the campus organizer who allows you to demonstrate.--John Hagee

I never had time.--Ulysses S. Grant in response to a question about if he ever felt fear on the battlefield

It is an unfortunate fact that we can secure peace only by preparing for war.--John F. Kennedy

We must not be enemies. Though passion may have strained, it must not break our bonds of affection. The mystic chords of memory, stretching from every battlefield and patriot grave, to every living heart and hearth-stone, all over this broad land, will yet swell the chorus of the Union when again touched, as surely they will be, by the better angels of our nature.--Abraham Lincoln

Leadership is a combination of strategy and character. If you must be without one, be without the strategy.--Norman Schwartzkopf

I may be compelled to face danger, but never fear it, and while our soldiers can stand and fight, I can stand and feed and nurse them.
--Clara Barton

So long as we have enough people in this country willing to fight for their rights, we'll be called a democracy.--Roger Baldwin

We confide in our strength, without boasting of it; we respect that of others, without fearing it.--Thomas Jefferson

Victories that are easy are cheap. Those only are worth having which come as the result of hard fighting.--Henry Ward Beecher

I think that almost all Americans want the best for our men and women in arms. I believe that's true for those who oppose the war-- a few crazies aside --as well for those who think the war is justified. --Joanne Jacobs[4]

All those who served during the Vietnam years hold clear that each of us did our job and had, for the most part, no control over what position we were given or where we were stationed. Each who did serve is special and a brother veteran.--Christopher Ward[5]

I do not believe there is any chance of us surviving the first push. I am proud to be trusted with such a post of honor and have the greatest confidence in my own men to do their duty to the end. --Hamilton Fish, Jr. during World War I

Whether we like it or not, the precedent that the United States might act decisively against regimes that were both suspected of pursuing WMD acquisition and doing nothing to allay those fears, has had a powerful prophylactic effect in the neighborhood. --Victor Davis Hanson

Only America has both the power and the optimism to defend the international community against what really are forces of darkness. --William Shawcross

The strength of our nation is measured by the character of the men and women who are in uniform.--Jodi Rell

In war, the objective must be only to win, and the Torah understands this.--Rabbi Daniel Lapin

Duty is the sublimest word in our language. Do your duty in all things. You cannot do more. You should never wish to do less. --Robert E. Lee

If the Vietnamese people were so mistreated by American soldiers, why was the United States the number-one destination of the thousands who fled when the communists took over South Vietnam?--B. G. Burkett[6]

We are soldiers who devote ourselves to arms not for the invasion of other countries but for the defense of our own, not for the gratification of our own private interest, but for the public security.--Nathanael Greene

Those who expect to reap the blessings of freedom must undergo the fatigue of supporting it.--Thomas Paine

Courage is the price that life exacts for granting peace. --Amelia Earhart

We are the most powerful nation in the world. Our involvement in that world, for better or for worse, is unavoidable.--Suzanne Terrell

Courage is the ladder on which all the other virtues mount. --Clare Booth Luce

The force that fought in Vietnam was America's best educated and most egalitarian in the country's history.--B. G. Burkett[7]

They are just going to have to kill me...I'm just not going to renounce my government or shame my people.--Colonel Fred Cherry, the first Black Vietnam POW whom the Vietnamese expected to renounce racist America, but despite twice a day torture he remained resolute[8]

With a good conscience our only sure reward, with history the final judge of our deeds, let us go forth to lead the land we love. --John F. Kennedy

The only thing necessary for the triumph of evil is for good men to do nothing.--Edmund Burke

Humility must always be the portion of any man who receives acclaim earned in the blood of his followers and the sacrifices of his friends.--Dwight D. Eisenhower

Evil cannot be accommodated. It must be defeated.--Cal Thomas[9]

That wall in Washington would be double in size if it wasn't for the medics, the dustoff choppers, and everybody who gave so much of themselves.--Kathy Lynn Emanuelsen[10]

To me protesting government policy was legitimate; traveling to North Vietnam and making broadcasts saying you supported the people trying to kill Americans and destroy a democratic nation was nothing short of collaborating with the enemy.--B. G. Burkett[11]

Every unit I was with went out of their way to be kind and decent with the people.--Peter Arnett on the Vietnam War

Born on the Fourth of July and *Platoon* share common characteristics. Both are laced with enough fact to make the stories difficult to refute while at the same time they are saturated with so much hateful negativism that in the end the proper term to describe them is probably "propaganda" or "disinformation."--Richard Eilert. [12]

Most of them--regardless of what they said--were primarily motivated by not having their lives interrupted.--William Smith a lawyer who helped many draft dodgers during the Vietnam War. [13]

America united with a handful of troops, or without a single soldier, exhibits a more forbidding posture to foreign ambition than America disunited, with a hundred thousand veterans ready for combat.--James Madison

This is the time to fight terrorism, not to walk away or be terrified by terrorism.--Colin Powell

Ours is a world of nuclear giants and ethical infants.
--Omar Bradley

Each and every one of the Vietnam memorials in that cemetery and in every other...belongs to a man who may have died in my place, and that is something that I can never put behind me.
--Mark Helprin, who successfully avoided the draft[14]

Draftees were less guilty than volunteers of violating military rules and regulations and had fewer problems with drugs.
--George Q. Flynn regarding Vietnam War-era soldiers[15]

It took a great deal of intellectual firepower over the course of the forty-year Cold War to help bring about the demise of the Soviet Union and the repudiation of the communist ideology upon which it was built. To maintain citizen support, our current war against terrorism will require nothing less.--William Bennett

There are risks and costs to action. But they are far less than the long-range risks of comfortable inaction.--John F. Kennedy

In war there is no substitute for victory.--Douglas MacArthur

Among the men who fought on Iwo Jima, uncommon valor was a common virtue.--Chester W. Nimitz

It is our duty still to endeavor to avoid war; but if it shall actually take place, no matter by whom brought on, we must defend ourselves. If our house be on fire, without inquiring whether it was fired from within or without, we must try to extinguish it.
--Thomas Jefferson

"Victims?" These men and women were not victims. They were the best and the brightest of my generation. They were warriors, patriots. Some of them were heroes!--B. G. Burkette on those who fought the Vietnam War[16]

A lot of people wouldn't want to see that, but I felt it was the least I could do for these men who were giving their lives and limbs for America.--Brenda Lee on visiting the hospitals in Vietnam[17]

Our enemies may be irrational, even outright insane, driven by nationalism, religion, ethnicity, or ideology. They do not fear the United States for its diplomatic skills or the number of automobiles and software programs it produces. They respect only the firepower of our tanks, planes, and helicopter gunships.
--Ronald Reagan

America was born on the battlefield. Our union was preserved by a Civil War. During World War II and the Cold War, our way of life was protected by armed might. Thus it will always be.--Don Feder[18]

It doesn't take a hero to order men into battle; it takes a hero to be one of those men who goes into battle.--Norman Schwarzkopf

Free men of the world are marching together to victory. I have full confidence in your courage, devotion to duty, and skill in battle. We will accept nothing less than full victory. Good luck, and let us all beseech the blessings of Almighty God upon this great and noble undertaking.--Dwight D. Eisenhower

The dead are husbands, wives, fathers, daughters, best friends, and for those who knew them in that capacity the loss is grievous. But Americans know them only as warriors, and they should honor them as such.--Mark Steyn[19]

My boy's death makes a liar out of Paul Robeson who said the Negro would never fight for their country against the Communists. --Van Charlton the father of Sergeant Cornelius H. Charlton, who was killed in action during the Korean War[20]

My mind drifts back to a dozen acts of supreme courage that I had witnessed in Vietnam, of tenderness shown by fearsome looking men to village children whose older brothers had planted mines and booby traps.--Morley Safer

Peace is generally good in itself, but it is never the highest good unless it comes as the handmaid of righteousness; and it becomes a very evil thing if it serves merely as a mask for cowardice and sloth, or as an instrument to further the ends of despotism or anarchy.--Theodore Roosevelt

I can never forget how thrilled I was at the sight of the Statue of Liberty.--Eugene Jacque Bullard, coming home from World War I[21]

The blood of our fathers--let it not have been shed in vain. --Daniel Webster

The men I saw over there were amazing. Their morale was better than it has been portrayed, but they didn't like what they heard from home.--Barbara Mandrell on entertaining troops in Vietnam [22]

Wars are fought only by people and leaders who believe that what they have is worth fighting for, and if need be dying for.
--Craige McMillan[23]

I have never advocated war except as a means of peace.
--Ulysses S. Grant

It is crucial that we maintain steady support within this nation, calling its citizens to the defense of its highest ideals and virtues.
--William Bennett

If history teaches us anything, it teaches that simple-minded appeasement or wishful thinking about our adversaries is folly.
--Ronald Reagan

Few of the quotes found in the preceding pages referenced the Korean War, but the servicemen who fought there were no less valiant, dedicated, or deserving of our thanks than those who waged any other military campaign. Eugene Chin Yu, Senior Vice President of Commercial & Military Systems, is one grateful American who is truly cognizant of the sacrifices made on behalf of the cause of freedom and knows well how these efforts directly benefited the innocent citizens of his native land during that conflict He expressed his heartfelt thanks at a commemorative ceremony held jointly by the Sarasota and Manatee (Florida) Counties Korean War Commemoration Committees on March 9, 2003. Here is an abbreviated version of his stirring speech that ably communicates sentiments so many feel toward veterans of all American wars.

Remarks by Eugene Chin Yu in tribute to Korean War Veterans March 9, 2003

Good morning, distinguished and honored guests, ladies and gentlemen, it is with pleasure and great pride that I stand before you this morning to honor the Korean War Veterans who fought for the freedom we enjoy so much today. My name is Eugene Chin Yu. I trust my beliefs, which I express to you in words today, are shared by all Korean Americans living across the United States today.

This year we are commemorating the 50th anniversary of the start of the Korean War. When North Korean Communists attacked South Korea quickly the American Armed Forces, along with their U.N. Allies responded by fighting alongside the (South) Korean Armed Forces in the air, on the ground, as well as at sea. These forces would make many sacrifices before the fighting was over.

The Expression of our recognition and gratitude for these American forces, along with our U.N. allies is long overdue. Young American men and women were wounded and died on Korean soil for Korea and for people they did not even know. Most young soldiers didn't even know where Korea was. They fought because their government called them to fight, but most importantly they fought for democracy, human rights, freedom, and against communism. They were the first military force to fight communism face-to-face, hand-to-hand. They prevailed. They drew a line in the sand at the 38th parallel and said to communism and the world: "No further!"

This was the first big step in the eventual fall of the Cold War that ended in 1990. You Korean War Veterans are the ones that made that big step. Therefore, I salute you for a duty well done! Many did not return to the loved ones they left behind, and those who did not return home were never able to enjoy the bounties of peace and freedom in the nation they had so honorably served.

I am reminded of men like you in your late teens and early twenties. You were young, good looking, with sparkling eyes, with no fear, healthy, (and) ready to fight wherever called. The bitter cold weather and terrain, lessons on hardship, sacrifice, the sight of death, and even the pure high risk adventure were never to be matched in your later life experiences. You are now older but still good looking and your eyes sparkle with pride at being here today.

Once again Korean War Veterans, families and spouses, it is time for us Koreans who became American citizens to express from our hearts our love to the people who made it possible for us to be here in America. We as Korean Americans clearly understand and know what the red stripes in the American Flag symbolize, the blood shed not only in Korea but (in) all the wars fought since the beginning of these United States of America for freedom around the world. Down through the years the backbone of our country has been made up from the people who emigrated from other countries like us Koreans. To many in other lands the American Dream still exists as a beacon of light that shines for freedom and hope in their lives--for them and their children.

I was born July 27 1953, 8 pm. People used to call me peace baby or peace boy, because I was born right after the war was over. I am Korean by birth, but I am also a strong flag-waving American citizen. We enjoy the freedom this American Flag has brought to us Koreans and so many others of our generation. My two children were born in Augusta, Georgia and are proud Americans, and may they always enjoy the freedom you made possible. Without you I would not be here today. Without me my children

14

would not be here today.

We are the example to the world. I'm not saying we are perfect, but in this country we have democracy, opportunity, freedom, and the best form of government at any level. Some Americans complain about America, but I tell you, we are far better off than being anywhere else in the world. You veterans built this country!

Other countries and other people say negative things about us. In some countries they show open hostility. Whenever they are in trouble they expect us to help them. We not only help them, we give our blood. Soon after their problems go away, they forget about us. Not only forget-- they talk (badly) about us. These same people depend on us to buy their products. We are the largest importer of goods and services in the world. These same people marvel at our ingenuity, watch our television and movies, and send their children to our colleges and universities. You, the Veterans of the Korean War, in sustaining this great country, helped provide the irresistible force for these people to embrace our cultural advancements that we share with the world today.

President John F. Kennedy said, "it is as true now today as veterans you serve with equal tenacity, devoting brain and heart to the task of keeping our country strong. All American Veterans share a special common bond of experience forged in sacrifice and danger for the benefit of every citizen in this great country." Thank you Veterans!

I am proud to be part of what being an American stands for. The strength of our country's foundation was built brick by brick. It started at Valley Forge and continued through the modern technology of warfare in Desert Storm and most recently in Operation Iraqi Freedom. The great American General Douglas MacArthur, who is known by all Koreans as a Korean War hero--I would like to quote from his speech after taking the Japanese surrender aboard the USS Missouri on September 2, 1945. He condemned the war in these terms:

If we will not devise some greater and more equitable system, Armageddon will be at our door. The problem basically is theological and involved a spiritual revival and improvement for human character that will synchronize with our almost

15

matchless advances of the past two thousand years.

Mankind is still searching for spiritual revival and (the) improvement of human characteristics. We can only hope that future generations of young men and women like you in 1950 will not have to endure but appreciate the freedom that you have helped to give us. In (General MacArthur's) last address to the United States Congress he said that, "old soldiers never die, they just fade away." In the hearts and minds of the Korean people, those young men and women who fought for our cause will never, "fade away," but will remain forever young, vibrant, and brave. As long as the Korean nation endures, they will always be remembered.

Fifty years have now passed since the start of the Korean War. When I look into the eyes of you veterans now I see the eyes of a 20-year-old fighting in Korea. It is a feeling of back to the future. As time passes forward I may never see you again in this lifetime, but we will meet again someday in an everlasting, eternal world. I want you to know that you will always be loved and remembered on behalf of all the boys and girls you saved during the Korean War.

Thank you for all you did. Thank you for the freedom you protected for us.

God bless you and God bless America!

JUSTICE

Justice is the end of government. It is the end of civil society. It ever has been and ever will be pursued until it be obtained, or until liberty be lost in the pursuit.--James Madison

In much of the world the idea of justice is chimerical; it simply does not exist. Unprovoked arrests, imprisonments, property confiscations, torture, even executions are done on the whims of the ruling authorities.

Standards and procedures such as arrest warrants, the right to a free attorney, appeals, innocent until proven guilty, the right to confront one's accuser, and humane treatment of prisoners are parts of the fabric of American jurisprudence. Most, if not all, are nonentities in many nations today.

In America a mere accusation of arbitrary racial profiling rightly earns widespread scorn and an official investigation. In many other countries minorities have no rights. Enduring as a subordinate class is a way of life for millions of people whose only "crime" was being born in the wrong country at the wrong time.

Of course the wheels of American justice are not perfect. We have seen too many cases of criminals getting off on technicalities and examples of activist judges twisting the law to satisfy their own predilections, knowing that diffident legislators will likely grin and bear their legal legerdemain. Yet, unlike the citizenry of other countries, Americans through sedulous toil can legally right any wrong we encounter, thanks to the inviolable judicial system our Founders devised.

In spite of its inherent flaws, it is safe to say the petty criminals and prisoners of conscience incarcerated in Libya, China, Sierra Leone, Somalia, or Vietnam would give anything for a taste of American judicial treatment--the fairest system known to mankind.

The bedrock of American justice is the Constitution--a document that changed the world more than any other. James Madison truly wrote a magnificent guide for the ages the day he scrolled that brief blueprint for freedom and prosperity.

Every quote in this section helps to spotlight the majesty of America's rule of law, and several pay tribute to the seminal genius codified in the United States Constitution.

The strength of the Constitution lies entirely in the determination of each citizen to defend it. Only if every single citizen feels duty bound to do his share in this defense are the constitutional rights secure.--Albert Einstein

We will not be satisfied until justice rolls down like waters and righteousness like a mighty stream.--Martin Luther King, Jr.

A judge who believes the Pledge of Allegiance is unconstitutional doesn't belong on the bench.--Dick Armey

It will be worthy of a free, enlightened, and at no distant period, a great nation to give to mankind the magnanimous and too novel example of a People always guided by an exalted justice and benevolence.--George Washington

When the law loses, freedom languishes.--Robert Kennedy

Without justice, courage is weak.--Benjamin Franklin

Let us not forget what the Constitution represents and for what it stands. The principles found in the Constitution should not be abused or liberalized. These principles must last for all generations.--Susan L. Boyd[1]

The trouble with "living constitutions" is that of necessity they end up having no meaning other than whatever meaning judges read into them. Dead--or "enduring"--constitutions can be changed but they must change by popular consent.--Jonah Goldberg[2]

We demand that big business give the people a square deal; in return we must insist that when anyone engaged in big business honestly endeavors to do right he shall himself be given a square deal.--Theodore Roosevelt

The best laws are understandable and they're evident to everyone, not just to those with legal training, as the common sense, moral way to do things. --Rod Paige

At the foundation of our civil liberties lies the principle that denies to government officials an exceptional position before the law and which subjects them to the same rules of conduct that are commands to the citizen.--Louis Brandeis

I believe that justice is instinct and innate, the moral sense is as much a part of our constitution as the threat of feeling, seeing and hearing.--Thomas Jefferson

The overriding objective of any national security policy should be national security.--Paul Greenberg[3]

Hold on to the Constitution, for if the American Constitution should fail, there will be anarchy throughout the world.--Daniel Webster

Wherever there is a human being, I see God-given rights inherent in that being, whatever may be the sex or complexion.--William Lloyd Garrison

The Constitution itself, plainly written as it is, the safeguard of our federative compact, the offspring of concession and compromise, binding together in the bonds of peace and union this great and increasing family of free and independent States, will be the chart by which I shall be directed.--James Polk

Dr. Martin Luther King is proof enough that great men do follow the rule of law and not the rule of man.--Roy Moore

In civil trials, let the plaintiffs demonstrate the injury and its cause directly to the judge and jury without any intervening testimony about the unknowable truth of their claims by psychoexpert witnesses. Let welfare applicants demonstrate their inability to work without the misbegotten advocacy of clinic experts.--Dr. Margaret A. Hagen[4]

People of good godly character make good godly laws.--Mike Huckabee[5]

If in the opinion of the people, the distribution or the modification of the constitutional powers be in any particular wrong, let it be corrected by an amendment in the way which the Constitution designates, but let there be no change by usurpation for though this in one instance may be the instrument of good, it is the customary weapon by which free governments are destroyed.--George Washington.

He who is permitted by law to have no property of his own, can with difficulty conceive that property is founded in anything but force.--Thomas Jefferson

Courts are the mere instruments of the law, and can will nothing. Judicial power is never exercised for the purpose of giving effect to the will of the Judge; always for the purpose of giving effect to the will of the law.--John Marshal

It is proper to kill a combatant during a war unless he surrenders first. It does not matter whether the combatant is a cook or bombmaker, a private or a general. Nor does it matter whether he wears an army uniform, a three-piece suit, or a kaffiyeh. So long as he is in the chain of command, he is an appropriate target regardless of whether he is actually engaged in combat at the time that he is killed or is fast asleep. Of course, his killing would be extra-judicial. Military attacks against combatants are not preceded by jury trials or judicial warrants.--Alan Dershowitz[6]

For mere vengeance I would do nothing. This nation is too great to look for mere revenge. But for the security of the future I would do everything.--James A. Garfield, with sad irony on the assassination of Abraham Lincoln

With the law cut down, none of us has anywhere to stand.--Paul Craig Roberts and Lawrence M. Stratton[7]

No power on earth has a right to take our property from us without our consent.--John Jay

Progress will take place when the Federal judiciary is made up of judges who believe in law and order and a strict interpretation of the Constitution.--Ronald Reagan

The limitation of riots, moral questions aside, is that they cannot win and their participants know it. Hence, rioting is not revolutionary but reactionary because it invites defeat. It involves an emotional catharsis, but it must be followed by a sense of futility.--Martin Luther King, Jr.

Arbitrary power and the rule of the Constitution cannot both exist. They are antagonistic and incompatible forces, and one or the other must of necessity perish whenever they are brought into conflict. --George Sutherland

The American system has uniquely nurtured justice and right. The idea enunciated in the Declaration of Independence that all men are created equal, has, for example, been a driving force behind the changes we have made to achieve a greater degree of equality than exists anywhere else in the world.--Lynne Cheney[8]

The future of this land is in our hands.--Steven McDonald[9]

It is the duty of a citizen not only to observe the law but to let it be known that he is opposed to its violation.--Calvin Coolidge

American offenders should surely be judged by our standards, not by others'.--Charles Krauthammer[10]

No man can suffer too much, and no man can fall too soon, if he suffers or if he falls in defense of the liberties and Constitution of his country.--Daniel Webster

There is nothing stable but Heaven and the Constitution.--James Buchanan

He that cannot obey cannot command.--Benjamin Franklin

I challenge us to remember that the greatness of a nation is not only measured in military might and certainly not by the rights and protections afforded to the most affluent. Rather, the greatness of a nation is measured by its might tempered with the respect, rights, and protections it affords to the least and most vulnerable of its people.--Kelly Hollowell[11]

The Declaration of Independence is literally the birth certificate for our Nation, but the United States was forming months and even years before its delivery on July 4th, 1776. Life truly did (and does) begin at conception.--Wesley Allen Riddle[12]

The history of liberty is the history of due process. When there is widespread contempt for the presumption of innocence in any case--leading to a prejudiced jury--our system of justice has become perverted.--William O. Douglas

Equal Rights for all, special privileges for none.--Thomas Jefferson

As the Declaration of Independence states, governments are legitimate only when they represent the consent of the governed.--Edwin Meese[13]

We have the good fortune, under the blessing of a benign Providence, to live in a country which we are proud of for many things--for its independence, for its public liberty, for its free institutions, for its public spirit, for its enlightened patriotism; but we are also proud--and it is among those things we should be the most proud of--we are proud of its public justice, of its sound faith, of its substantially correct morals in the administration of Government, and the general conduct of the country since she took her place among the nations of the world.--Daniel Webster

It's time for all of us to stand up for our country, for our kids, for our cops.--Stephen McDonald[14]

The storm of frenzy and faction must inevitably dash itself in vain against the unshaken rock of the Constitution.--Franklin Pierce

The Constitution, on this hypothesis, is a mere thing of wax in the hands of the Judiciary, which they may twist and shape into any form they please.--Thomas Jefferson

The First Amendment says nothing about a right not to be offended. The risk of finding someone else's speech offensive is the price each of us pays for our own free speech.--Jeff Jacoby[15]

The ultimate measure of a man is not where he stands in moments of comfort and convenience, but where he stands at times of challenge and controversy.--Martin Luther King, Jr.

Do not separate text from historical background. If you do, you will have perverted and subverted the Constitution.--James Madison

The Supreme Court is divided almost in half on the decisions. Talk about an international court. How would we ever agree with a lot of foreigners when we can't even agree among our own judges?--Will Rogers

The Constitution of the United States is not a mere lawyers' document: it is a vehicle of life, and its spirit is always the spirit of the age.--Woodrow Wilson

Don't interfere with anything in the Constitution. That must be maintained, for it is the only safeguard of our liberties.--Abraham Lincoln

Our Constitution was made only for a moral and religious people. It is wholly inadequate to the government of any other.--John Adams

The American constitutions were to liberty, what a grammar is to language: they define its parts of speech, and practically construct them into syntax.--Thomas Paine

The American concept of Justice is largely derived from principles articulated so succinctly and sublimely in our Constitution. Sadly, while all functioning Americans can readily name the document, too many are not well-versed with its genuine content--including know-it-all throngs who claim to be experts in what it says and attribute the most outlandish positions to its text. For over 200 years James Madison's superb composition has successfully served as a guide for the freest nation on earth. The following lecture eloquently pays tribute to America's judicial blueprint. The John M. Ashbrook Center for Public Affairs Executive Director Peter W. Schramm profoundly delineates why a mastery of the Constitution is essential for productive American citizenship. He fittingly delivered these remarks on September 17, 1997 which many Americans would probably not be able to identify as Constitution Day.

Remembering That We Are A Constitutional People On Principle
by: Peter W. Schramm

September 17, 1997. Constitution Day. It was on this day two hundred and ten years ago when the Constitutional Convention that had gathered in Philadelphia adjourned, the delegates having voted to recommend to their fellow citizens the Constitution they had spent the hot summer in writing. This was seen as a momentous act. Some great deed had been accomplished, the likes of which had not been seen before. By 1789 enough states had ratified the Constitution to allow it to go into effect.

On this day in the contemporary world if the Constitution is mentioned at all it is mentioned only because some public opinion poll has learned that few people know anything about it. We are bombarded with statistics about the fact that most people don't know who their Congressman is; that most do not know that each state, regardless of population, has two Senators; that most people can't identify "We the People of the United States, in order to form a more perfect Union..." as the beginning of the document. And we are reminded of other facts of

25

which we are ignorant.

Yet, during these same days, we are trying to bring democratic government to countries from Haiti to China to Bosnia. And we think this is a good thing, even if done at the point of a gun. After all, isn't it true that if you asked any high school senior what form of government the United States has, he would invariably answer, we are a democracy?

It's bad enough that citizens do not know facts about the Constitution; what is worse is that they have almost no appreciation of its purpose. What is the Constitution for? After all, if we wanted a democracy, we could have instituted one. We could have had a simple regime in which the majority, ruling directly, would have governed. But we did not do that. And there are good reasons for this.

This day should remind us that majority rule (or democracy) is an incomplete understanding of what we ourselves are (and also of what we would like other countries to become). In fact we are more of a constitutional people than a democratic one.

We do not deny that the majority have a right to rule. We affirm that all human beings are born free and equal and have natural rights. But we think that this power of the people is limited: government, even when that government is based on the people's consent, has no right to take away those rights that human beings have by nature. Government didn't give us those rights and government has no right to take them away. Indeed, we have established government so that those rights may be more secure.

The proposed Constitution of 1787, and the fact that it was ratified by the thirteen states, reflects well on the mind and character of the American nation. In ratifying the Constitution the people did nothing less than place formal limits on their own power. They did something that they could have avoided doing. They could have willfully argued that because they had a right to rule, the majority could do whatever it wanted. But they did not argue this. Indeed, both the proponents and the opponents of the Constitution argued that the government had to be limited. The majority— through the Constitutional provisions of separation of powers, checks and balances, federalism, etc.—saw that it was necessary to make itself as reasonable and moderate as possible. The purpose was to create good government based on, in Hamilton's words, "reflection and choice" rather than "accident and force."

It is one of the most amazing facts in the history of the world that a people, calling themselves a nation since 1776, and having established their legitimate right to rule on universal grounds of right, should immediately limit their own power. They recognized that the rule of the majority should be made republican and constitutional else they would end up ruling only in its own interest. And they also understood that habits of self-government, guided by the formalities of the Constitution, had to be maintained if the people were to remain free.

We have forgotten much of this because we have been bombarded, unfortunately, over the span of this century with a strange ideological view of the Constitution that argues that it is a living, growing document; that it can become whatever we want it to become; that it can, and should, accommodate itself to the peculiarities and perversities of any particular age; that it is so flexible that it means nothing. The Constitution, thus runs the argument, just gets in the way of our will, interest, and passion. It is nothing but an inconvenience. It interferes with our democratic passions.

But James Madison, the Father of the Constitution, whom Thomas Jefferson in 1790 called "the greatest man in the world," would disagree with us. He and the other Founding Fathers would ask us to reconsider our willfully ignorant ways, to remember the enduring purpose of the Constitution, and thereby to ennoble our civic lives immeasurably.

FREEDOM

We must be willing to pay a price for
freedom.--H. L. Mencken

The notion of freedom is innate to native-born Americans because we have never been without it. Even those familiar with current events-- who understand the horrors of many oppressive regimes across the globe-- fail to fully absorb just how blessed we are to enjoy our copious American liberties.

Our basic freedoms (speech, religion, peaceful assembly, the press, etc.) evinced so distinctly in the Constitution are mere pipe dreams in many dictatorships and are severely constrained in many ostensibly democratic countries. Canada is a place not normally associated with draconian restrictions of basic rights, but people there who utter the wrong remarks risk up to five years in prison. In France, another nation thought of as progressive and tolerant, freedom of the press is similarly abridged. A few years ago a reporter who wrote an unflattering story about the French president and one of his previous wives, faced the threat of punitive charges for the offense.

In the United States the thought of such abridgements is laughable. Assaults on freedom of speech not too infrequently appear on radical college campuses under the current fad of curtailing "hate speech." Fortunately, these violations of the First Amendment are generally deemed unconstitutional by a court when opposition to them needs to proceed so far. Such outrageous measures could never stand judicial scrutiny because they stand in stark contrast to the precepts enunciated in the Bill of Rights.

America's freedom of religion is similarly enshrined to the point that it feels natural. In 2002 an activist court catered to the demands of one pushy atheist who wanted to remove the phrase "under God" from the Pledge of Allegiance. So insulting was the judicial machination that the Unites States Senate--in a rare bipartisan gesture--voted unanimously to condemn the illicit ruling, and the US Supreme Court reversed the travesty. In 2005 a contradictory set of Supreme Court rulings said that the Ten Commandments cannot be displayed in courthouses--except when they can be? The Justices simultaneously handed down these conflicting fiats in plain view of a fresco of Moses with the Decalogue that adorns their chambers. Regardless of some Supreme Court poppycock, the Supreme Being still has a welcome place in America, and the freedom to worship as one pleases still thrives here too.

Many of our immigrants know what a lack of freedom of religion is. In several Islamic countries a radical stream of the sect mandates the death penalty for conversion to other creeds. Saudi Arabia is said not to have a single church within its boundaries. China sponsors house churches--state controlled institutions where the tenets of the faith are supplanted by communist dogma. In France the stereotypical bastion of liberalism most religious symbols and attire including crucifixes and Islamic headscarves are outlawed in public schools. In Israel, the Jewish State, Jews are routinely targeted for murder by Islamic terrorists while much of the worldwide community denounces any retaliation or even reasonable efforts at prevention.

Despite the slanted, ratings-craving news favored by today's network anchors, freedom of the press flourishes in the United States. Yet the practice is rare around the world. In Iran a journalist was condemned to death for publishing a poll that showed a large majority of the population wished to resume negotiations with America. Fortunately, outraged masses caused the tepid, power-clutching mullahs to rescind the execution, but many other voices of truth have not been so lucky. In Russia, long after the Soviet Union collapsed, newspapers advocating opposition parties have been shut down by government decree.

Young lives have been sacrificed throughout American history so that we can enjoy our American liberties--sacred freedoms unknown to most of the world.

The quotes here pay tribute to our healthy liberties and honor those who gave their lives so that America can forever remain the Last Best Hope on Earth.

Guard with jealous attention the public liberty.--Patrick Henry

Freedom is the natural condition of the human race, in which the Almighty intended men to live.--Abraham Lincoln

A constitution of government once changed from freedom, can never be restored. Liberty, once lost, is lost forever. --John Adams

To limit an individual's education is to limit his freedom. A sound education is the fastest, and sometimes the only, way out of poverty.--Gerald Reynolds

Without liberty, law loses its nature and its name, and becomes oppression. Without law, liberty also loses its nature and its name, and becomes licentiousness.--James Wilson

I know no class of my fellowmen, however just, enlightened, and humane, which can be wisely and safely trusted absolutely with the liberties of any other class.--Fredrick Douglass

They that can give up essential liberty to obtain a little temporary safety deserve and receive neither liberty nor safety.--Benjamin Franklin

Our country is in danger, but not to be despaired of. Our enemies are numerous and powerful; but we have many friends, determining to be free, and heaven and earth will aid the resolution. On you depend the fortunes of America. You are to decide the important question, on which rest the happiness and liberty of millions yet unborn. Act worthy of yourselves. --Joseph Warren

The flames kindled on the 4th of July 1776, have spread over too much of the globe to be extinguished by the feeble engines of despotism; on the contrary, they will consume these engines and all who work them.--Thomas Jefferson

Our defense is in the preservation of the spirit which prizes
liberty as the heritage of all men, in all lands, everywhere.
--Abraham Lincoln

The sound of tireless voices is the price we pay for the right to
hear the music of our own opinions.--Adlai Stevenson

If you love wealth more than liberty, the tranquility of servitude
better than the animating contest of freedom, go home from us
in peace. We ask not your counsel or arms. Crouch down and
lick the hands which feed you. May your chain be set lightly
upon you and may posterity forget ye were our countrymen.
--Samuel Adams

In [American] society, you know that sometimes it's important to
sacrifice yourself or other cherished things for the principle of
liberty.-- Khaled Abou El Fadl

Liberty lies in the hearts of men and women; when it dies there,
no constitution, no law, no court can save it.--Learned Hand

We, and all others who believe in freedom as deeply as
we do, would rather die on our feet than live on our knees.
--Franklin Delano Roosevelt

We are all better off to be living in a country where freedom for
all individuals is the law of the land.--Jesse Helms

Those who profess to favor freedom, and yet depreciate
agitation, are men who want crops without plowing up the
ground.--Frederick Douglass

I would rather be exposed to the inconveniences attending
too much liberty than to those attending too small a degree
of it.-- Thomas Jefferson

Freedom and dignity of the individual have been more assured here than any other place on earth.--Ronald Reagan

Liberty, when it begins to take root, is a plant of rapid growth.
--George Washington

A day--an hour--of virtuous liberty is worth a whole eternity of bondage.--Joseph Addison

America 'from sea to shining sea' (is) the greatest country in the world, 'the land of the free and the home of the brave' and I was lucky to have been born there.--Norman Podhoretz[1]

Liberty is worth whatever the best civilization is worth.
--Henry Giles

Liberty is always dangerous, but it is the safest thing we have.
--Henry Emerson Fosdick

Liberty cannot be preserved without a general knowledge among the people, who have... a right, an indisputable, unalienable, indefeasible, divine right to that most dreaded and envied kind of knowledge, I mean the characters and conduct of their rulers.--John Adams

So far as a person thinks; they are free.--Ralph Waldo Emerson

The tree of liberty must be refreshed from time to time with the blood of patriots and tyrants.--Thomas Jefferson

The truth is: all might be free if they valued freedom and defended it as they ought.--Samuel Adams.

Our country offers the most wonderful example of democratic government on a giant scale that the world has ever seen; and the peoples of the world are watching to see whether we succeed or fail.--Theodore Roosevelt

In regard to foreign policy, I would deal with nations as equitable law requires individuals to deal with each other, and I would protect the law-abiding citizen, whether of native or foreign birth, wherever his rights are jeopardized or the flag of our country floats. I would respect the rights of all nations, demanding equal respect for our own. If others depart from this rule in their dealings with us, we may be compelled to follow their precedent.--Ulysses S. Grant

God grants liberty only to those who love it, and are always ready to guard and defend it.--Daniel Webster

I believe there are more instances of the abridgement of the freedom of the people by gradual and silent encroachments of those in power than by violent and sudden usurpations.
--James Madison

The limits of tyrants are prescribed by the endurance of those whom they oppress.-- Frederick Douglass

The right to freedom being the gift of God, it is not in the power of man to alienate this gift and voluntarily become a slave.--Samuel Adams

I had reasoned this out in my mind, there was one of two things I had a right to, liberty or death; if I could not have one, I would have the other.--Harriet Tubman

Without morals a republic cannot subsist any length of time.
--Charles Carroll

Democracy is two wolves and a lamb voting on what to have for lunch. Liberty is a well-armed lamb contesting the vote!
--Benjamin Franklin

What light is to the eyes--what air is to the lungs--what love is to the heart, liberty is to the soul of man.--Robert Green Ingersoll

Every nation has learned - or should have learned - an important lesson: freedom is worth fighting for, dying for and standing for - and the advance of freedom leads to peace. Liberty is both the plan of heaven for humanity, and the best hope for progress here on earth.--George W. Bush

We are right to take alarm at the first experiment upon our liberties.--James Madison

The very aim and end of our institutions is just this: that we may think what we like and say what we think.
--Oliver Wendell Holmes

I would rather belong to a poor nation that was free than to a rich nation that had ceased to be in love with liberty.
--Woodrow Wilson

The boisterous sea of liberty is never without a wave.
--Thomas Jefferson

A general dissolution of the principles and manners will more surely overthrow the liberties of America than the whole force of the common enemy.--Samuel Adams

Liberty is slow fruit. It is never cheap; it is made difficult because freedom is the accomplishment and perfectness of man.--Ralph Waldo Emerson

History does not long entrust the care of freedom to the weak or the timid.--Dwight Eisenhower

Where justice is denied, where poverty is enforced, where ignorance prevails, and where any one class is made to feel that society is in an organized conspiracy to oppress, rob, and degrade them, neither persons nor property will be safe.--Frederick Douglass

Liberty consists in wholesome restraint.--Daniel Webster

Arbitrary power is like most other things which are very hard, very liable to be broken.--Abigail Adams

It surprises me that every man does not rally at the sound of liberty and array himself with those who are laboring to abolish slavery in our country.--Dr. Harris (first name unknown), a Revolutionary War veteran

Liberty has never come from the government. Liberty has always come from the subjects of the government. The history of government is a history of resistance. The history of liberty is the history of the limitation of government, not the increase of it.--Woodrow Wilson

Men may die, but the fabrics of free institutions remains unshaken.--Chester A. Arthur.

The history of the world proves that our liberties and opportunities are unlike any others that have been ever known to man, regardless of empire or dynasty. The opportunities that we enjoy today should be defended and protected for future generations.--Ak'Bar Shabazz[2]

If my name ever goes into history, it will be for this act. --Abraham Lincoln on the Emancipation Proclamation

The shallow consider liberty a release from all law, from every constraint. The wise man sees in it, on the contrary, the potent Law of Laws.--Walt Whitman

If we pursue security to the point where we give up that which makes us Americans, the enemy has won.--James Gilmore

Independence is happiness.--Susan B. Anthony

The preservation of the sacred fire of liberty and the destiny of the republican model of government are justly considered... deeply...finally staked on the experiment entrusted to the hands of the American people.--George Washington in his first inaugural address

The second day of July 1776 will be the most memorable epocha in the history of America.--John Adams, not realizing that it would take two more days to ratify the Declaration of Independence

Let us rise up tonight with a greater readiness. Let us stand with greater determination. And let us move in these powerful days, these days of challenge, to make America what it ought to be. --Martin Luther King, Jr.

Timid men prefer the calm of despotism to the tempestuous sea of liberty.--Thomas Jefferson

Those are the same stars, and that is the same moon, that look down upon your brothers and sisters, and which they see as they look up to them, though they are ever so far away from us, and each other.--Sojourner Truth

National honor is national property of the highest value. --James Monroe

He that would make his own liberty secure, must guard even his enemy from oppression; for if he violates this duty, he establishes a precedent that will reach to himself.--James Wilson

Freedom is the open window through which pours the sunlight of the human spirit and human dignity.--Herbert Hoover

Rights carry responsibilities. Freedom is no license to hurt other people. That which is wrong may be a right, but it is not right to do.--Tonya Flynt-Vega[3]

Is life so dear or peace so sweet as to be purchased at the price of chains and slavery? Forbid it!--Patrick Henry

To fight for liberty requires selfless conviction.--David Wienir[4]

Freedom and liberty will triumph, sooner than you think.
--Murray Sabrin

Freedom is not divisible. If people can be trusted to invest and manage material assets, they will eventually ask why they cannot be trusted with decisions over what to say and what to believe.
--Dick Cheney

The spirit of 1776 spread freedom all over the world.
--C. Mason Weaver[5]

The American's Creed: I believe in the United States of America as a government of the people, by the people, for the people, whose just powers are derived from the consent of the governed; a democracy in a Republic; a sovereign Nation and many sovereign States; a perfect Union, one and inseparable; established upon those principles of freedom, equality, justice, and humanity for which American patriots sacrificed their lives and fortunes. I therefore believe it is my duty to my country to love it, to support its Constitution, to obey its laws, to respect its Flag, and to defend it against all enemies.
--William Tyler Page

The Founders held not only that freedom is the foundation of just law, but that freedom leads also to the maximization of prosperity, happiness, and individual virtue in a society.
--Bret Schundler

As American freemen we can not but sympathize in all efforts to extend the blessings of civil and political liberty, but at the same time we are warned by the admonitions of history and the voice of our own beloved Washington to abstain from entangling alliances with foreign nations.--Zachary Taylor

I have long believed that the guiding hand of Providence did not create this new nation of America for ourselves alone, but for a higher cause: the preservation and extension of the sacred fire of human liberty. The Declaration of Independence and the Constitution of these United States are covenants we have made not only with ourselves, but with all of mankind. Our founding documents proclaim to the world that freedom is not the sole prerogative of a chosen few, they are the universal right of all God's children.--Ronald Reagan

Individual liberty is individual power, and as the power of a community is a mass compounded of individual powers, the nation which enjoys the most freedom must necessarily be in proportion to its numbers the most powerful nation. --John Quincy Adams

Last Monday a string of amendments were presented to the lower house; these altogether respect personal liberty.--William Grayson on the Bill of Rights

Let us renew our commitment to standing for life, and liberty, and peace for all people. Let us renew our commitment to working with all nations to conquer want, and hunger, and disease in every corner of the globe. Let us accept our responsibility to defend the freedom which we are so privileged to enjoy.--Condoleezza Rice

In America we rightly cherish our freedoms because we are aware of just how rare such liberties are. Sadly savvy demagogues sometimes speciously invoke our basic freedoms (speech, peaceful assembly, the press etc.) to augment their own agenda. As the following composition trenchantly elucidates, freedom of speech does not mean one has a right to speak irresponsibly in a public forum and remain free from criticism or rebuke. Envelope-pushing comic Bill Maher made some asinine remarks shortly after September 11, 2001, and as an American citizen he certainly had every right to do so. No rational voice ever denied him that Constitutionally guaranteed prerogative. When his hateful prattling brought forth widespread denunciation and censure that eventually forced his network to cancel his program, he falsely claimed that his freedom of speech was being violated. A few commentators (including some who should know much better) mistakenly came to his defense. In reality those who pilloried Maher were merely exercising their own more thoughtful freedom of speech back at him.

Adam Cirucci's reasoned dialectic perfectly shows that our precious freedom of speech does not include a freedom of consequence from offensive statements and also includes the right for others to convey "shut up" if they take offense at what we say. The essay also subtly highlights just how blessed we are to be living in a nation that allows unfettered expression of even unpopular or controversial opinion. Freedom comes with certain responsibilities, and each of us must be willing to face the response to whatever our words or actions provoke.

This piece was originally published by Accuracy in Media on June 25, 2002.

Bill Maher and the First Amendment
by Adam Cirucci

Bill Maher's five-year run on ABC will come to an end this week when *Politically Incorrect* airs its last episode on June 28. Maher has been in hot water since September 17, when he commented that the U.S. military was cowardly in comparison with the warrior hijackers of 9/11.

Needless to say, Maher's comments were met with national criticism, but despite the immediate backlash, various writers and pundits have come to his defense. DeWayne Wickham, Arianna Huffington, and David Horowitz have argued that Maher's removal infringes upon his First Amendment rights.

Maher's statements came in response to President Bush's reference to the 9/11 terrorism as a "faceless coward." Within hours of the attack, Bush vowed to "hunt down and punish those responsible for these cowardly acts" and in a subsequent joint resolution of Congress, the suicide hijackings were termed "heinous and cowardly." Thankfully, however, Maher stepped forward to ensure that our government did not unjustly label the 9/11 terrorists. After days of around-the-clock coverage from Ground Zero, Maher decided to go on television and say, "We have been the cowards, lobbing cruise missiles from 2,000 miles away. That's cowardly. Staying in the airplane when it hits the building, say what you want about it, it's not cowardly."

Of course, Maher received much criticism. Although others agreed with him (Dinesh D'Souza, Arianna Huffington, and Susan Sontag all denied the essential cowardice of suicide-bombers), their comments were either worded better or better timed. Maher was the first to come out and say it and say it in a particularly tactless way. Under pressure from ABC, Maher apologized for his comments the next night. Despite, his explanation and apology, however, FedEx, Sears and General Motors immediately dropped *Politically Incorrect*. And now ABC has dropped Maher.

What is wrong with that? The host of a national talk show made a serious blunder, companies withdrew their accounts from the show (resulting in an estimated $10 million loss) and the station canceled it. A lot of shows get canceled.

Yet somehow, critics argue that canceling *PI* undermines Maher's freedom of speech. Horowitz wrote, "*Politically Incorrect* may be the first casualty of the war against terrorism. This would be a travesty of the war effort and a blow to freedom in this country." In late September, Huffington, a frequent *PI* guest and Maher friend, began circulating an online petition titled, "In Support of Bill Maher." The petition reads, "We consider such [attempts to silence Mr. Maher] to be blatantly un-American and will not support any such attempts by sponsors or ABC."

While Maher's comments may have triggered a semantic and philosophical debate over the meaning of "courage," his removal has absolutely nothing to do with the First Amendment. No one has prevented him from speaking his mind. Maher can go out and voice his opinion on any street corner or forum.

Just not on ABC. Maybe Maher and friends ought to be reminded that speech on television is not free. Television is a business. Maher's removal is about as un-American as capitalism. Sure, he has the right to speak his mind, but networks reserve the right to cut his show. Likewise, companies reserve the right to advertise where they see fit. So, if a show is unpopular, businesses are not reaching their customers and a station is losing money, the show will probably be canceled.

That is just the case with *Politically Incorrect*. The show was not doing well: Maher had already been in trouble for referring to an ailing Ronald Reagan as "nuts" and equating retarded children with dogs. Then, less than a week after the collapse of the World Trade Center and during an unprecedented anthrax scare, Maher questioned the courage of our nation. Obviously, this is a delicate subject. Even if the name of your show is *Politically Incorrect*, this argument needs to be approached gracefully.

But Maher failed. Regardless of the validity of his argument, he angered viewers and cost the network money. Consequently, ABC found a preferable comedian (Jimmy Kimmel) to fill the late night slot. That is capitalism. Anything else would be un-American.

SEPTEMBER 11

America has become a better place because of that attack.--Dennis Prager[1]

     September 11, 2001. The date says it all. Like December 7, 1941, it is a date that will live in infamy. Nearly 2,900 of our fellow citizens were brutally slaughtered, and our murdered brothers and sisters were far from the only victims. Family members left behind will never fully recover. Millions endure physical and/or emotional wounds, many industries suffered devastating financial hits, and as Americans we were all violated. The utter effrontery of such unbridled evil sent shockwaves through every citizen and all decent people worldwide. The indescribable savagery that befell America seriously wounded us, but terrorism signed its own death warrant that day.

     We all knew--even if we could never bring ourselves to consciously admit it--that New York City was a terrorist's dream target. Our society is so open, so free, so successful, so inviting, so welcoming, so enviable; it is everything that the terror masters fear and hate--knowing that they can never equal. Yet, this latent awareness of the potential danger did not prepare us for the terrible day.

     Washington, DC is home to the government that understandably evokes jealousy in every other nation on earth. We all complain about our politicians and the federal bureaucracy, but no other nation enjoys our freedom, opportunity, or security thanks to our sometimes infuriating government. The desirability of our governmental hub as a terror target was also not difficult to divine, but the obvious feasibility of such a strike did not lessen our horror when it finally happened nearby at the Pentagon.

     There were innumerable heroes that day and many of their deeds will never be known in this life. Those in the towers or the Pentagon who aided or comforted coworkers or strangers--many of whom did not get out alive themselves--the firemen, policemen, and other rescuers who did their job as unquestionably that day as they routinely do, the people on flight 93 who mutinied against their hijackers and saved untold lives by thwarting phase four of the terrorists' diabolical plot. In the face of such inexorable turmoil, these great Americans inspired us all. Their courageous actions will stand eternally as potent exemplifications of the undefeatable American Spirit.

The United States--although gravely wounded--grew stronger because of September 11. Osama Bin Laden did more to unite us as a nation than anyone else in world history ever did. The wicked terrorists thought that they would score a decisive blow against "the Great Satan," but today they are hiding under rocks and running for their worthless lives. September 11 served as the impetus to free 50,000,000 of their fellow citizens in Afghanistan and Iraq and the liberating winds of freedom have started to blow throughout the Middle East. They thought America would shrink and revert to the backward ways of their part of the world. Now thanks to our just retaliation their part of the world is starting--however slowly--to simulate America's lofty path.

Many of the quotes in this section illuminate how unified we were by the incursions, and how so much good came out of such unfathomable evil. Of course we wish that we had been able to prevent the attacks, but America has displayed a noble resoluteness beyond anyone's wildest imagination. Although never forgetting the loved ones we lost, we shall endure and prevail. To the terrorists everlasting nightmare The United States of America is prouder, stronger, and freer than ever!

Interestingly, many of the included quotes that so emphatically apply to September 11 were uttered by Americans long before the attacks. Some of the speakers died over a hundred years before 2001, but their messages resonated loudly that day and in the ensuing battles that have followed. In our darkest moment not only were modern Americans joined as one, but the encouraging words left behind by many who had gone before nurtured our wounded spirit and suggest that they would be very proud of our ongoing response.

What an example New York and Washington have been to the world these past few days! None of us will ever forget the pictures of our courageous firefighters and police, many of whom have lost friends and colleagues, or the hundreds of people attending or standing patiently in line to donate blood. A tragedy like this could have torn our country apart, but instead it has united us and we've become a family.--Billy Graham

The city is going to survive, we are going to get through it. It's going to be (a) very, very difficult time. I don't think we yet know the pain that we're going to feel when we find out who we lost, but the thing we have to focus on now is getting this city through this, and surviving and being stronger for it.--Rudolph Giuliani

From every walk of life, from every ethnic, racial background, New Yorkers came together with unbelievable heroism. And you know, the message to the rest of the country is maybe we talk too fast at times, maybe we're a very opinionated people, but when the crisis comes, there are no stronger people, no people more willing to sacrifice and stand together in defense of America and defense of our freedom than New Yorkers.--George Pataki

Our Nation is at war, our economy is in recession, and the civilized world faces unprecedented dangers. Yet the state of our Union has never been stronger.--George W. Bush

Face it America. There will be more terrorist strikes against the homeland, not because our government is incompetent, but because evil is relentless.--David Thibault

I totally support my family's statement that expressed condolences and deepest sympathy for the victims of the attack and unequivocally denounced and condemned the attacks and all those behind them. --Abdullah Mohammed Binladin, Boston resident and Osama Bin Laden's brother

Let's Roll!--Todd Beamer

We have only one path open to us that can bring some semblance of peace and security to the innocent men, women, and children of the United States. We must obliterate every trace of the terror network wherever it is. We must find and destroy them using every means at our disposal. And we must be merciless.--Mona Charen[2]

Right now, our country faces a great challenge as we seek to successfully combat terrorism. I fully support President Bush's efforts to achieve that goal.--Al Gore, less than a year after losing a brutal presidential race.

We once were a nation of neighbors and friends, we are again today. We once were a nation of hardship-tested dreamers, we are again today. We once were a nation under God, we are again today. Our enemies attacked one nation, they will encounter another. For they underestimated us. Today in our grief and in our rage our determination and hope, we've summoned what's best and noblest in us-we are again Americans.--Tony Snow

Pat Tillman represented what is best about America.--Ben Shapiro[3]

Since September 11, our perspectives have changed; the lens through which we look at the world around us, at each other, has altered. What we took for granted yesterday, we see with new eyes-perhaps clearer eyes-today. What was commonplace to us yesterday, we think about in new ways today. And that's one of the reasons we deliberately chose to convene this Summit in New York City, not in defiance, but as a tribute to the city's resilience. Simply put, we have a new definition of what "normal" means, and we're all struggling to wrap our minds around it.--Charles Curie

Even in horror there is beauty to be seen, even in trauma there is strength to be gained, and at the heart of every defeat is the seed of a future victory.--Peggy Noonan[4]

This was not only an attack on America, it was an attack on Islam, the Koran, and on every Muslim.--Shaykh Muhammad Hisham Kabbani, Chairman of the Islamic Supreme Council of America

Our country was attacked and we can no longer rely on the oceans to protect the safety of our shores and our people, but through these difficult days, America has emerged more resolved and more united. --Mel Martinez

Those who seek to separate us will now see us closer to each other. --Rabbi Joseph Potasnik

Not to punish mass murder is to acquiesce to evil.--Don Feder[5]

We cannot predict the length or the course of the conflict, but we know with absolute certainty that this nation will persevere, and we will prevail.--Dick Cheney

Our precious world is threatened by twisted minds who think the way to heaven is to murder innocent civilians. We have only one chance to live a normal life. We have to look this evil in the eye and defeat it. Not passively and sluggishly. But with the same degree of passion, and the same level of commitment, that the evil is being waged against us. Every human being has a personal responsibility to fight this epidemic. --Rabbi Noah Weinberg[6]

What makes this tragedy so despicable is that people commit these atrocities in the name of God. As a Muslim, I say to you: any human being who can support these attacks has lost their humanity.--Azhar Usman

Our enemies have made the mistake that America's enemies always make. They saw liberty and thought they saw weakness. And now, they see defeat.--George W. Bush

Millions of Americans wish they could be here tonight with us. They saw the Twin Towers fall, and watched helplessly, wanting to do something to defend America and our way of life.--Capt. Ronald H. Henderson Jr. before leading troops into battle in Afghanistan.[7]

We have to make the cost to the governments that support terrorism so high that they stop supporting them.--Richard N. Perle

I speak on behalf of my entire nation when I say: today we are all Americans--in grief, as in defiance.--Binyamin Netanyahu, September 24, 2002

We American Muslims must retain perspective. Who are the real villains? The frightened, victimized American public, or the terrorists who are murdering innocent people in our name, and in the name of our God?--Marlon Mohammed[8]

Having conquered the criminal chaos and financial insolvency of the last decade, recovering from the homicidal attacks of al-Queda will in many ways be much simpler.--Karl Zinsmeister on New York City.[9]

Ultimately there is just one way to secure the homeland, and that is by destroying the enemy.--Jeff Jacoby[10]

The men and women who died in the World Trade Center came from nations all over the world, but the rescuers came from the USA. --William Donahue

To those who masterminded this cruel plot, and to those who carried it out...the spirit of this nation will not be defeated by their twisted and diabolical schemes.--Billy Graham

In the aftermath of the terrorist attack on September 11, 2001, Iranians gathered in large numbers and held candlelight vigils while chanting slogans in support of and sympathy for America.--Reza Pahlavi, son of the last Shah of Iran

There was a glittering city, the greatest in the history of man, a place of wild creativity, of getting, grabbing, and selling, of bustle and yearning and greed. It was brutally attacked by a band of primitives. The city reeled. We knew what to expect: The selfish, heartless city-dwellers would trample children in their path as they raced for safety, they'd fight for the lifeboats like the wealthy on the *Titanic*. It didn't happen. It wasn't that way at all. They were better than they knew! They saved each other--they ran to each other's aid, they died comforting strangers.--Peggy Noonan[11]

We resolved a year ago to honor every person lost. We owe them remembrance, and we owe them more. We owe them, and their children, and our own, the most enduring monument we can build: A world of liberty and security made possible by the way America leads, and by the way Americans lead our lives.--George W. Bush, September 11, 2002

There's no question that we as a country are much more united, much more willing to express our patriotism and not feel self conscious about it. There were people who were afraid that the country would forget and become complacent, but I go all around the country...and people remember.--Rudy Giuliani

If we in this country have learned anything the past year, it's that whatever the ethnic modifier that happens to dangle in front of the hyphen (before 'American'), we know we're all in this together now-- whether as the bull's-eye for the world's crazy, embittered people or indeed as the project of common national purpose conceived by the Founding Fathers.--Daniel Henninger[12]

I have heard people say that what has happened to America is our own fault, that we have offended people with our foreign policies and indifference to the third world countries. Of course, that's the biggest bunch of junk ever to spill forth from the collective mouths of these idiots.--Charlie Daniels

We can't let the evil ones dictate how we live our lives. Rather, we must decisively take whatever action is necessary to insure that these murderous cowards who live to kill, and long to die, achieve the latter before the former.—J. Matt Barber[13]

Yes, many. As a matter of fact, I lost 2,752 of my wonderful fellow humans.--Elbert Shamsid-Dean, when asked if he lost anybody on September 11

Now, we have inscribed a new memory alongside those others. It's a memory of tragedy and shock, of loss and mourning. But not only of loss and mourning. It's also a memory of bravery and self-sacrifice, and the love that lays down its life for a friend--even a friend whose name it never knew.--George W. Bush

Bomb the hell out of them.—Zell Miller

Terrorists have no religion. Terrorists have agendas--and we categorically reject their agenda. Islam regards terrorism as a cowardly and predatory act against God and man.--Ahmed Umar Abdallah,

These heroes died defending their families and ours, and protecting our homeland from murder and attack.--Donald Rumsfeld, about flight 93 that crashed in Pennsylvania

They gave me a good time in Cuba. They were very nice to me, giving me English lessons. The Americans were so nice to me.--Mohammed Ismail Agha, 15-year-old released Guantanamo Bay detainee

They treated us well. We had enough food. I didn't mind [being detained] because they took my old clothes and gave me new clothes. --Faiz Mohammed, an elderly Afghan farmer who was detained at Guantanamo Bay for eight months before being released

The one unchangeable certainty is that nothing is unchangeable or certain.--John F. Kennedy

Join hand in hand, brave Americans all! By uniting we stand, by dividing we fall.--John Dickinson

Even though we face the difficulties of today and tomorrow, I still have a dream.--Martin Luther King

I congratulate the country upon the fraternal spirit of the people and the manifestations of good will everywhere so apparent. --William McKinley

Any jackass can kick a barn down, but it takes a carpenter to build it. --Sam Rayburn

We must be constantly prepared for the worst and constantly acting for the best.--Lyndon Johnson

You can run, but you cannot hide.--Ronald Reagan

The American people are slow to wrath, but when their wrath is once kindled it burns like a consuming flame.--Theodore Roosevelt

Tyranny, like hell, is not easily conquered; yet we have this consolation with us, that the harder the conflict, the more glorious the triumph.--Thomas Paine

We (Americans) have a way of pulling through and pushing on, and the blood of the men and women who have gotten us through our rocky past beats within us still; it is our patrimony and our inspiration. --Ronald Reagan

The world is a dangerous place to live; not because of the people who are evil, but because of the people who don't do anything about it. --Albert Einstein

Since the end of Cold War, Soviet aggression had been replaced by a number of particularly venomous threats, from Timothy McVeigh to Osama bin Laden.--Barbara Olson, who was killed on September 11, 2001 on board flight 77 that crashed into the Pentagon[14]

Fundamentally, public opinion wins wars.--Dwight Eisenhower

The dogmas of the quiet past are inadequate to the stormy present. The occasion is piled high with difficulty, and we must rise with the occasion. As our case is new, so we must think anew and act anew. --Abraham Lincoln

The American eagle may be slow to anger but once incensed nothing can stand against it.--David Schippers[15]

We must take a stand against terrorism in the world and combat it with firmness, for it is a most cowardly and savage violation of peace. We must remember our heritage, who we are and what we are, and how this nation, this island of freedom, came into being.--Ronald Reagan

If, by the grace of God, we stand steadfast in our great traditions through this time of stress, we shall insure that we and our sons and daughters shall see these fruits increased many fold.--Herbert Hoover

In the uncertain days right after September 11, most of us felt like zombies as we tried to carry on with our lives the best way that we could. We knew that our world forever changed on the bright sunny late summer morning but were not really sure how to cope or where to turn. America's collective heart was broken and we desperately needed some sense of security back in our lives.

Although President George W. Bush updated the nation regularly from the night of the eleventh, it was not until September 20, that he spoke to a joint session of Congress in a high-stakes, internationally scrutinized speech. The bipartisan sentiments he relayed palliated a badly wounded nation and the powerful oratory seems somewhat prophetic in hindsight. The unprecedented unity of our ever-bickering elected officials helped us all realize that America would endure, and a long campaign to eradicate terrorism would soon commence. Much has happened since that time. The national cohesion and president's overwhelming popularity have diminished greatly as petty squabbles have once again leapfrogged into prominence on the American political stage. While at one level the quarreling is unfortunate, it also proves that America did recover and things did return to normal. We have moved forward with a newfound cognizance of the magnitude of the evil that we face. The president's serious words--addressing the crisis of a moment in 2001--ably express the timeless resolve of many Americans as we fight the protracted war on terror.

Remarks by President George W. Bush to a joint session of congress on September 20, 2001

Mr. Speaker, Mr. President Pro Tempore, members of Congress, and fellow Americans: in the normal course of events, Presidents come to this chamber to report on the state of the Union. Tonight, no such report is needed. It has already been delivered by the American people.

We have seen it in the courage of passengers, who rushed terrorists to save others on the ground--passengers like an exceptional man named

Todd Beamer. And would you please help me to welcome his wife, Lisa Beamer, here tonight. We have seen the state of our Union in the endurance of rescuers, working past exhaustion. We have seen the unfurling of flags, the lighting of candles, the giving of blood, the saying of prayers--in English, Hebrew, and Arabic. We have seen the decency of a loving and giving people who have made the grief of strangers their own.

My fellow citizens, for the last nine days, the entire world has seen for itself the state of our Union--and it is strong. Tonight we are a country awakened to danger and called to defend freedom. Our grief has turned to anger, and anger to resolution. Whether we bring our enemies to justice, or bring justice to our enemies, justice will be done.

I thank the Congress for its leadership at such an important time. All of America was touched on the evening of the tragedy to see Republicans and Democrats joined together on the steps of this Capitol, singing "God Bless America." And you did more than sing; you acted, by delivering $40 billion to rebuild our communities and meet the needs of our military.

Speaker Hastert, Minority Leader Gephardt, Majority Leader Daschle and Senator Lott, I thank you for your friendship, for your leadership and for your service to our country.

And on behalf of the American people, I thank the world for its outpouring of support. America will never forget the sounds of our National Anthem playing at Buckingham Palace, on the streets of Paris, and at Berlin's Brandenburg Gate. We will not forget South Korean children gathering to pray outside our embassy in Seoul, or the prayers of sympathy offered at a mosque in Cairo. We will not forget moments of silence and days of mourning in Australia and Africa and Latin America.

Nor will we forget the citizens of 80 other nations who died with our own: dozens of Pakistanis; more than 130 Israelis; more than 250 citizens of India; men and women from El Salvador, Iran, Mexico and Japan; and hundreds of British citizens. America has no truer friend than Great Britain. Once again, we are joined together in a great cause--so honored the British Prime Minister has crossed an ocean to show his unity of purpose with America. Thank you for coming, friend.

On September the 11th, enemies of freedom committed an act of war against our country. Americans have known wars--but for the past 136 years, they have been wars on foreign soil, except for one Sunday in 1941. Americans have known the casualties of war--but not at the center of a great city on a peaceful morning. Americans have known surprise attacks--but never before on thousands of civilians. All of this was brought upon us in a single day--and night fell on a different world, a world where freedom itself is under attack.

Americans have many questions tonight. Americans are asking: Who attacked our country? The evidence we have gathered all points to a collection of loosely affiliated terrorist organizations known as al-Qaeda. They are the same murderers indicted for bombing American embassies in Tanzania and Kenya, and responsible for bombing the USS Cole. Al-Qaeda is to terror what the mafia is to crime. But its goal is not making money; its goal is remaking the world--and imposing its radical beliefs on people everywhere.

The terrorists practice a fringe form of Islamic extremism that has been rejected by Muslim scholars and the vast majority of Muslim clerics-- a fringe movement that perverts the peaceful teachings of Islam. The terrorists' directive commands them to kill Christians and Jews, to kill all Americans, and make no distinction among military and civilians, including women and children.

This group and its leader--a person named Osama bin Laden--are linked to many other organizations in different countries, including the Egyptian Islamic Jihad and the Islamic Movement of Uzbekistan. There are thousands of these terrorists in more than 60 countries. They are recruited from their own nations and neighborhoods and brought to camps in places like Afghanistan, where they are trained in the tactics of terror. They are sent back to their homes or sent to hide in countries around the world to plot evil and destruction.

The leadership of al-Qaeda has great influence in Afghanistan and supports the Taliban regime in controlling most of that country. In Afghanistan, we see al-Qaeda's vision for the world. Afghanistan's people have been brutalized--many are starving and many have fled. Women are not allowed to attend school. You can be jailed for owning a television. Religion can be practiced only as their leaders dictate. A man can be jailed in Afghanistan if his beard is not long enough.

The United States respects the people of Afghanistan--after all, we are currently its largest source of humanitarian aid--but we condemn the Taliban regime. It is not only repressing its own people, it is threatening people everywhere by sponsoring and sheltering and supplying terrorists. By aiding and abetting murder, the Taliban regime is committing murder.

And tonight, the United States of America makes the following demands on the Taliban: Deliver to United States authorities all the leaders of al-Qaeda who hide in your land. Release all foreign nationals, including American citizens, you have unjustly imprisoned. Protect foreign journalists, diplomats, and aid workers in your country. Close immediately and permanently every terrorist training camp in Afghanistan, and hand over every terrorist, and every person in their support structure, to appropriate authorities. Give the United States full access to terrorist training camps, so we can make sure they are no longer operating. These demands are not open to negotiation or discussion. The Taliban must act, and act immediately. They will hand over the terrorists, or they will share in their fate.

I also want to speak tonight directly to Muslims throughout the world. We respect your faith. It's practiced freely by many millions of Americans, and by millions more in countries that America counts as friends. Its teachings are good and peaceful, and those who commit evil in the name of Allah blaspheme the name of Allah. The terrorists are traitors to their own faith, trying, in effect, to hijack Islam itself. The enemy of America is not our many Muslim friends; it is not our many Arab friends. Our enemy is a radical network of terrorists, and every government that supports them. Our war on terror begins with al-Qaeda, but it does not end there. It will not end until every terrorist group of global reach has been found, stopped and defeated.

Americans are asking, why do they hate us? They hate what we see right here in this chamber--a democratically elected government. Their leaders are self-appointed. They hate our freedoms--our freedom of religion, our freedom of speech, our freedom to vote and assemble and disagree with each other.

They want to overthrow existing governments in many Muslim

countries, such as Egypt, Saudi Arabia, and Jordan. They want to drive Israel out of the Middle East. They want to drive Christians and Jews out of vast regions of Asia and Africa. These terrorists kill not merely to end lives, but to disrupt and end a way of life. With every atrocity, they hope that America grows fearful, retreating from the world and forsaking our friends. They stand against us, because we stand in their way.

We are not deceived by their pretenses to piety. We have seen their kind before. They are the heirs of all the murderous ideologies of the 20th century. By sacrificing human life to serve their radical visions--by abandoning every value except the will to power--they follow in the path of fascism, and Nazism, and totalitarianism. And they will follow that path all the way, to where it ends: in history's unmarked grave of discarded lies.

Americans are asking: How will we fight and win this war? We will direct every resource at our command--every means of diplomacy, every tool of intelligence, every instrument of law enforcement, every financial influence, and every necessary weapon of war--to the disruption and to the defeat of the global terror network. This war will not be like the war against Iraq a decade ago, with a decisive liberation of territory and a swift conclusion. It will not look like the air war above Kosovo two years ago, where no ground troops were used and not a single American was lost in combat.

Our response involves far more than instant retaliation and isolated strikes. Americans should not expect one battle, but a lengthy campaign, unlike any other we have ever seen. It may include dramatic strikes, visible on TV, and covert operations, secret even in success. We will starve terrorists of funding, turn them one against another, drive them from place to place, until there is no refuge or no rest. And we will pursue nations that provide aid or safe haven to terrorism. Every nation, in every region, now has a decision to make. Either you are with us, or you are with the terrorists. From this day forward, any nation that continues to harbor or support terrorism will be regarded by the United States as a hostile regime.

Our nation has been put on notice: We are not immune from attack. We will take defensive measures against terrorism to protect Americans.

Today, dozens of federal departments and agencies, as well as state and local governments, have responsibilities affecting homeland security. These efforts must be coordinated at the highest level. So tonight I announce the creation of a Cabinet-level position reporting directly to me-- the Office of Homeland Security. And tonight I also announce a distinguished American to lead this effort, to strengthen American security: a military veteran, an effective governor, a true patriot, a trusted friend--Pennsylvania's Tom Ridge. He will lead, oversee and coordinate a comprehensive national strategy to safeguard our country against terrorism, and respond to any attacks that may come.

These measures are essential. But the only way to defeat terrorism as a threat to our way of life is to stop it, eliminate it, and destroy it where it grows. Many will be involved in this effort, from FBI agents to intelligence operatives to the reservists we have called to active duty. All deserve our thanks, and all have our prayers. And tonight, a few miles from the damaged Pentagon, I have a message for our military: Be ready. I've called the Armed Forces to alert, and there is a reason. The hour is coming when America will act, and you will make us proud.

This is not, however, just America's fight. And what is at stake is not just America's freedom. This is the world's fight. This is civilization's fight. This is the fight of all who believe in progress and pluralism, tolerance and freedom.

We ask every nation to join us. We will ask, and we will need, the help of police forces, intelligence services, and banking systems around the world. The United States is grateful that many nations and many international organizations have already responded--with sympathy and with support. Nations from Latin America, to Asia, to Africa, to Europe, to the Islamic world. Perhaps the NATO Charter reflects best the attitude of the world: An attack on one is an attack on all.

The civilized world is rallying to America's side. They understand that if this terror goes unpunished, their own cities, their own citizens may be next. Terror, unanswered, can not only bring down buildings, it can threaten the stability of legitimate governments. And you know what-- we're not going to allow it.

Americans are asking: What is expected of us? I ask you to live your lives, and hug your children. I know many citizens have fears tonight, and I ask you to be calm and resolute, even in the face of a continuing threat. I ask you to uphold the values of America, and remember why so many have come here. We are in a fight for our principles, and our first responsibility is to live by them. No one should be singled out for unfair treatment or unkind words because of their ethnic background or religious faith.

I ask you to continue to support the victims of this tragedy with your contributions. Those who want to give can go to a central source of information, libertyunites.org, to find the names of groups providing direct help in New York, Pennsylvania, and Virginia. The thousands of FBI agents who are now at work in this investigation may need your cooperation, and I ask you to give it.

I ask for your patience, with the delays and inconveniences that may accompany tighter security; and for your patience in what will be a long struggle. I ask your continued participation and confidence in the American economy. Terrorists attacked a symbol of American prosperity. They did not touch its source. America is successful because of the hard work, and creativity, and enterprise of our people. These were the true strengths of our economy before September 11th, and they are our strengths today. And, finally, please continue praying for the victims of terror and their families, for those in uniform, and for our great country. Prayer has comforted us in sorrow, and will help strengthen us for the journey ahead.

Tonight I thank my fellow Americans for what you have already done and for what you will do. And ladies and gentlemen of the Congress, I thank you, their representatives, for what you have already done and for what we will do together.

Tonight, we face new and sudden national challenges. We will come together to improve air safety, to dramatically expand the number of air marshals on domestic flights, and take new measures to prevent hijacking. We will come together to promote stability and keep our airlines flying, with direct assistance during this emergency. We will come together to give law enforcement the additional tools it needs to track down terror here at home. We will come together to strengthen our intelligence capabilities to know the plans of terrorists before they act, and find them before they strike. We will come together to take active steps that strengthen America's economy, and put our people back to work.

Tonight we welcome two leaders who embody the extraordinary spirit of all New Yorkers: Governor George Pataki, and Mayor Rudolph Giuliani. As a symbol of America's resolve, my administration will work with Congress, and these two leaders, to show the world that we will rebuild New York City.

After all that has just passed--all the lives taken, and all the possibilities and hopes that died with them--it is natural to wonder if America's future is one of fear. Some speak of an age of terror. I know there are struggles ahead, and dangers to face. But this country will define our times, not be defined by them. As long as the United States of America is determined and strong, this will not be an age of terror; this will be an age of liberty, here and across the world.

Great harm has been done to us. We have suffered great loss. And in our grief and anger we have found our mission and our moment. Freedom and fear are at war. The advance of human freedom--the great achievement of our time, and the great hope of every time--now depends on us. Our nation--this generation--will lift a dark threat of violence from our people and our future. We will rally the world to this cause by our efforts, by our courage. We will not tire, we will not falter, and we will not fail.

It is my hope that in the months and years ahead, life will return almost to normal. We'll go back to our lives and routines, and that is good. Even grief recedes with time and grace. But our resolve must not pass. Each of us will remember what happened that day, and to whom it happened. We'll remember the moment the news came--where we were and what we were doing. Some will remember an image of a fire, or a story of rescue. Some will carry memories of a face and a voice gone forever.

And I will carry this: It is the police shield of a man named George Howard, who died at the World Trade Center trying to save others. It was given to me by his mom, Arlene, as a proud memorial to her son. This is my reminder of lives that ended, and a task that does not end. I will not forget this wound to our country or those who inflicted it. I will not yield; I will not rest; I will not relent in waging this struggle for freedom and security for the American people.

The course of this conflict is not known, yet its outcome is certain. Freedom and fear, justice and cruelty, have always been at war, and we know that God is not neutral between them. Fellow citizens, we'll meet violence with patient justice--assured of the rightness of our cause, and confident of the victories to come. In all that lies before us, may God grant us wisdom, and may He watch over the United States of America.

Thank you.

IRAQ'S LIBERATION

If it was not for the American people and the sacrifices their sons and daughters have made, we would not see this day, a day where Saddam is in court and he's on the other side of the table, where he is the one who is being tried for his crimes.
--Tanya Gilly co-founder the Iraq-American Freedom Alliance

Those of us alive today will bear witness to few other undertakings that are as noble as the American led liberation of Iraq. As necessary and honorable as toppling the Taliban and freeing the Afghani populace was, Iraq's emancipation even surpasses that feat. In the post-September 11 world, leaving a wicked madman sitting on a powder keg is not a viable option, and America's own safety was rightly the primary reason for overthrowing Baghdad's butcher. Yet, the manumission of the oppressed Iraqi people was a joyous side effect.

Is there a person alive who didn't read a description of Saddam Hussein's savagery that won't be shaken by the details for the rest of his or her life? The rampant horrors in Iraq would have justified our invasion even if Saddam posed no threat to our own security. The civilized world cannot idly sit by while massacres of that magnitude take place. Some have correctly noted that similarly heinous acts are presently perpetrated in Sudan, China, North Korea, Cuba, and numerous other nations. Who knows what the future holds for any of those regimes?

Shortly after military operations commenced noticeable changes occurred beyond Iraq's boundaries. Libya's abandonment of its Weapons of Mass Destruction programs would never have taken place had Saddam's reign of terror been left unchecked. Syria's voluntary withdrawal from Lebanon after a decades-long occupation received minimal media fanfare (as the occupation itself had been afforded) but allowed the long-suffering Lebanese people to shake off the yoke of oppression. Kuwait's contemplation of allowing women to vote is a good sign, Saudi Arabia's recent municipal elections represent a mere baby step forward; however, it indicates significantly more progress than the sybaritic kingdom had previously demonstrated, and all marathons begin with a first step. Iran's government is still a menace but there will be no stopping its teeming dissident class. The brave Iranians are starting to evoke memories of Poland's 1980s Solidarity movement and their future--while certainly difficult--looks to be ultimately very bright indeed. None of these changes would be underway had Iraq not been liberated.

The lesson from Iraq is that the United States is serious in prosecuting the War on Terror. Additionally, the conduct of the military showed that the war is not against indigenous people who are daily victims of terrorist-sponsoring despots but against those who blithely eviscerate their own populations

All who lived through the liberation are better for having observed firsthand such a magnanimous undertaking. Those of us blessed to wear the label of "American" can feel a patriotic pride knowing it was our country that orchestrated the overthrow of a despicable tyrant and ended three decades of torture, rape, maiming, and summary executions for twenty-five million human beings.

The heroic battle that brought freedom to Iraq remains in progress as this book goes to press, and a growing unease toward the ongoing battle can be seen among the American population. Al-Qaeda and its allies horrific attacks against America's gallant troops and innocent Iraqis show the terrorists' desperation but have weakened the resolve of some decent Americans who shutter at the repeated manifestation of such uncivilized slaughter. It is a good thing that 24-hour news channels were not available during the Revolutionary War (where 4,435 American lives were lost), the Civil War (558,052), World War I (126,000) or World War II (350,000.) The problems, setbacks, and casualties of those conflicts--had they been repetitiously aired in American living rooms--would likely have prompted some serious reservations too. Yet America's record is not one of running when the going gets tough. Our military will emerge triumphant and leave behind a very loyal ally in a free and prospering Iraq. In spite of the best efforts of the barbarians, it is clear that an American victory is at hand. Good will defeat evil in another battle of the War on Terror.

As with the September 11 section, a few of these quotes were said years before action commenced in Iraq, but again it seems as though the speakers were exhibiting true prescience or else the cliché that history repeats itself is truer than ever.

For the first time in decades, Iraqis are truly free. More than 150 newspapers have been started since liberation. All major cities and 85 percent of towns now have a municipal council where Iraqis are increasingly taking responsibility for management of local matters.--Paul Bremer

The United Nations as an organization failed to help rescue the Iraqi people from a murderous tyranny that lasted over 35 years, and today we are unearthing thousands of victims in horrifying testament to that failure.--Hoshyar Zebari, Iraq's Interim Foreign Minister

We see our liberation as the start of a friendship with the U.S. and the U.K. that should last a thousand years. The U.S. and the U.K. showed that a friend in need is a friend indeed. Nothing can change that.--Khalid Kishtaini, Iraqi novelist

The tension is reducing every day. We are seeing a change. People are starting to realize that the soldiers are not here to occupy Fallujah forever; they're here to help us rebuild. --Taha Bedawi, Mayor of Fallujah,

I have great respect for the men and women fighting overseas to protect our way of life in Iraq and other parts of the world. As the son of an Army officer, I understand the strength, courage, and discipline required to successfully carry out their missions in hostile environments and feel tremendous pride they are representing us.--Tiger Woods

The government that emerges...will be decided by the free Iraqi people.--Donald Rumsfeld

This is a day we've been waiting for for 35 years...I'm very, very proud to be an American today, as well as an Iraqi. --Feisal Amin Al-Istrabadi, an American of Iraqi dissent

As his handler, I grew attached to him, but the reason I really wanted to see him in the States was because he supported us the whole time we were in Iraq.--Sergeant 1st Class Russell Joyce on the abused stray German Shepherd his unit adopted and who later obtained clearance to bring the dog home to the USA

Instead of shouting and criticizing the American initiative, you have to bring democracy to your countries, and then there will be no need to fear America or your people.--Seif al-Islam Gadhafi, Muammar Qaddafi's son

What you have done is immense. You have come from afar and delivered our people from injustice. You came to liberate our people. Mission accomplished.--Barham Salih, a leader of the Kurdish enclave

We will be with you in this fight for liberty. And if our spirit is right and our courage firm, the world will be with us.--Tony Blair

You represent all that is good and right about America and are the true face of American patriotism. You walk in those same righteous footsteps of all those patriots who, before you, fought to preserve liberty for all. Our prayers and our personal gratitude are with you and your families. May God Bless You. --Charlton and Lydia Heston.

You will be hard pressed to find a single family in Iraq which has not had a son, a father or brother killed, imprisoned, tortured or disappear due to Saddam's regime.--Rania Kashi, an Iraqi immigrant to England

Freedom is so very important. I can't express the feelings that overwhelmed me when I finally went out on the streets. My old friends were shocked when they saw me.--Ibrahim, (last name not provided) who hid in his mother's house for the last 23 years of Saddam's regime

Saddam Hussein was a weapon of mass destruction.
--Joseph Lieberman

A few speeches from moderate Muslims in Iraq thanking our
American troops and contractors for their service to the Arab
world would be well timed.--M. Zuhdi Jasser[1]

You cannot rebuild a city or country-a country destroyed by
war-in one month.--Mohammed Tahar al-Abid Rabu,
a member of the Mosul City Council

It's a chance to defend our country for our people. It's good to work
with the American soldiers. They give us new training and a mutual
respect.--Omar Abdullah, a recruit in Iraq's new army

The people of Iraq have demonstrated to the world what they think of
the regime and how grateful they are that that regime has been brought
to an end.--John Howard

We have full freedom to print anything we want. The coalition doesn't
interfere in our work but, of course, we have our own red lines.
--Ishtar el Yassiri, editor of an Iraqi newspaper

I'm 49, but I never lived a single day; only now will I start living.
--Imam Yusuf Abed Kazim after the fall of Saddam

It made it seem worthwhile.--Lance Cpl. Brian Cole, after
being handed a note by a 7-year-old Iraqi girl that read
"Thank you for liberate us. And thank you for help us.
You are a great army." (sic)

For the first time I feel really free.--Latif Yahia, Uday Hussein's former
double, after hearing of Uday's death

The argument that because America did not find a nuclear bomb in Saddam's closet the mass graves of innocent Iraqis don't qualify as sufficient motivation for defense from the outside--this is, in my opinion, a concerted effort to morally enfeeble our children, and that will not only weaken our country. It will make the world more available for evil to have a triumphant reign. --Laura Schlessinger[2]

It is like the soul coming back to the body.-- Ibrahim Abdullah, a refugee returning to Iraq

We're happy, we're rid of Saddam Hussein; the torture and executions of 35 years are over. We should wait to see what the Americans will do. --Ahmed Abdel-Sahib

Let us never forget that though war is a terrible thing, and there are innocent people that die as well as guilty people in a war; let us never forget that in the 30 years that Iraq was under the tyranny of Saddam, hundreds of thousands of people died in the most appalling and brutal circumstances.--Tony Blair

The US-led coalition should accept that the road ahead will be bumpy. But that is not necessarily bad news. For democracy is nothing but a journey on constantly bumpy roads.--Amir Taheri[3]

The pessimists and critics see the problems in Iraq and cling to old realities and old ways of doing things. In the face of terrorist acts, they seek retrenchment and retreat. They would dim the light of America's hope and promise.--Richard S. Williamson

The nightmare that Saddam Hussein has brought to the people of Iraq is ending. A new era is dawning in Iraq: for the first time in decades, the Iraqi people will experience freedom instead of fear . . . prosperity instead of persecution . . . and peace instead of cruelty and terror.--Samuel W. Bodman

Monsieur le President, don't you remember the landing in Normandy? Don't you know how many Americans died in Normandy to chase the nazis from France?--Oriana Fallaci[4]

The Iraqi people are happy now. It's the happiest moment in my life. It's my liberation day.--Salah Flaih, immigrant from Iraq

I can see that the American soldiers are free. In our old army, we were always under pressure and strict military orders. There was tough punishment.--Raad Mamoud, a former Iraqi soldier

Given what every intelligence agency on the planet agreed was going on in Iraq, the president made the right choice, indeed the only choice.--Charles Krauthammer[5]

Everyone fighting in Iraq and elsewhere is a professional who has voluntarily chosen a hazardous line of work. They deserve our gratitude and respect, not our pity.--James Taranto[6]

The names Uday and Qusay sent fear into the hearts of the Iraqi people. Now, thanks to the coalition forces, Iraqis are free of their terror.--Ayad Rahim, Iraqi-born American journalist[7]

We feel safer now because we used to hear lots of stories about girls. We were so afraid to go out in case Uday saw us.
--Farrah (last name not provided) a 15-year-old Iraqi girl

The liberation of Iraq was a brilliant and necessary act of initiative that demonstrated to the world that we as Americans, and our great allies, are united in our commitment to the protection of free people and the promotion of democracy our Founding Fathers envisioned.--Scott E Rutter[8]

They are happier that we are here.--2nd Lieutenant Tim Mayer

It's a relief; it's like a weight off my chest.--M. Mahdi, a member of the
Iraqi Republican Guard after being captured by US forces

While I cringe at one American death, so few comparatively
make a statement about the capabilities of this nation, our
military, and our intentions.--Tammy Bruce[9]

Those who question the wisdom of removing Saddam Hussein
from power, and liberating Iraq, should ask themselves: how
long should Saddam Hussein have been allowed to torture the
Iraqi people?--Condoleezza Rice

At the trial of Saddam, as at the trial of Adolf Eichmann in 1961,
the prosecutor will not stand alone. With him will stand hundreds
of thousands of silent accusers--the men, women, and children
whose voices were forever stilled during the long nightmare of
Saddam's reign but whose blood has never ceased crying out
from the ground.--Jeff Jacoby[10]

Iraq is also becoming a reflecting pool of the world at large.
Millions are slowly learning how different the United States is
from its critics in Europe.--Victor Davis Hanson[11]

We have wasted 75 years waiting to taste freedom.--Hadid al-Gailani

It's not as if anyone is worried that we're making a horrible
miscalculation and could be removing the Iraqi Abraham Lincoln
by mistake.--Ann Coulter[12]

If 5,000 Iraqi children were dying every month under Saddam,
and we have now been in Iraq one year, it means that 60,000
children have been saved. That's a number worth remembering.
--Helle Dale[13]

Americans don't shoot women and children. They don't kill
soldiers who have surrendered. That's what the &%#^ we're up
against do. That's what we're fighting.--Captain Adam Carson[14]

My anxious recollections, my sympathetic feeling, and my best wishes are irresistibly excited whensoever, in any country, I see an oppressed nation unfurl the banners of freedom.
--George Washington

The limits of tyrants are prescribed by the endurance of those whom they oppose.--Frederick Douglass.

If I could find a way to get [Saddam Hussein] out of there, even putting a contract out on him, if the CIA still did that sort of a thing, assuming it ever did, I would be for it.--Richard Nixon, during his presidency

Righteousness is easy in retrospect.--Arthur Schlesinger, Jr.

Peace, commerce, and honest friendship with all nations; entangling alliances with none.--Thomas Jefferson

Freedom is never voluntarily given by the oppressor; it must be demanded by the oppressed.--Martin Luther King, Jr.

Danger--if you meet it promptly and without flinching--you will reduce the danger by half. Never run away from anything. Never!--Winston Churchill

We are not to expect to be translated from despotism to liberty in a feather bed.--Thomas Jefferson

The time is near at hand which must determine whether Americans are to be free men or slaves.--George Washington

It is a common observation here that our cause is the cause of all mankind, and that we are fighting for their liberty in defending our own.--Benjamin Franklin

As the War in Iraq rages on and with the gallimaufry of always-available media outlets obsessing over the terrorist attacks, setbacks, explosions, killings, and other negatives, it is good to keep in perspective just what is at stake and that many advances are being made despite the very real, still present dangers. On September 23, 2003 Iraq's then-Interim Prime Minister Iyad Allawi addressed a join session of Congress where he offered the innocent Iraqi people's deep thanks for America's unselfish toil and spelled out the unglamorous progress that has been taking place throughout his beleaguered country. Since his visit, the media have maintained their focus on the steady stream of carnage, but Iraq has continued to move forward thanks to the steadfast resolve of doughty Iraqis and the protective friendship of some of America's finest.

Remarks by Interim Iraqi Prime Minister
Iyad Allawi on September 23, 2003

Mr. Speaker, Mr. Vice President, members of Congress, distinguished guests, it's my distinct honor and a great privilege to speak to you today on behalf of Iraq's interim government and its people. It's my honor, too, to come to Congress and to thank this nation and this people for making our cause your cause, our struggle your struggle.

Before I turn to my government's plan for Iraq, I have three important messages for you today. First, we are succeeding in Iraq. It's a tough struggle with setbacks, but we are succeeding. I have seen some of the images that are being shown here on television. They are disturbing. They focus on the tragedies, such as the brutal and barbaric murder of two American hostages this week. My thoughts and prayers go out to their families and to all those who lost loved ones. Yet, as we mourn these losses, we must not forget either the progress we are making or what is our stake in Iraq. We are fighting for freedom and democracy--ours and yours. Every day we strengthen the institutions that will protect our new democracy, and every day we grow in strength and determination to defeat the terrorists and their barbarism.

The second message is quite simple and one that I would like to deliver directly from my people to yours. Thank you, America. We Iraqis know that Americans have made and continue to make enormous sacrifices to liberate Iraq, to assure Iraq's freedom. I have come here to thank you and to promise you that your sacrifices are not in vain. The overwhelming majority of Iraqis are grateful. They are grateful to be rid of Saddam Hussein and the torture and brutality he forced upon us; grateful for the chance to build a better future for our families, our country and our region. We Iraqis are grateful to you, America, for your leadership and your sacrifice for our liberation and our opportunity to start anew.

Third, I stand here today as the Prime Minister of a country emerging finally from dark ages of violence, aggression, corruption, and greed. Like almost every Iraqi, I have many friends who were murdered, tortured or raped by the regime of Saddam Hussein. Well over a million Iraqis were murdered or are missing. We estimate at least 300,000 in mass graves, which stand as monuments to the inhumanity of Saddam's regime. Thousands of my Kurdish brothers and sisters were gassed to death by Saddam's chemical weapons. Millions more like me were driven into exile. Even in exile, as I myself can vouch, we were not safe from Saddam. And as we lived under tyranny at home, so our neighbors lived in fear of Iraq's aggression and brutality. Reckless wars, the use of weapons of mass destruction, the needless slaughter of hundreds of thousands of lives, and the financing and exporting of terrorism, these were Saddam's legacy to the world.

My friends, today we are better off, you are better off, and the world is better off without Saddam Hussein. Your decision to go to war in Iraq was not an easy one, but it was the right one. There are no words that can express the debt of gratitude that future generations of Iraqis will owe to Americans. It would have been easy to have turned your back on our plight, but this is not a tradition of this great country. Not for the first time in history, you stood up with your allies for freedom and democracy.

Ladies and gentlemen, I particularly want to thank you and the United States Congress for your brave vote in 2002 to authorize American men and women to go to war to liberate my country, because you realized what was at stake. And I want to thank you for your continued commitment last year when you voted to grant Iraq (a) generous reconstruction and security funding package. I have met many of you, last year, and I have in Iraq. It's a tribute to your commitment to our country that you have come to see firsthand the challenges and the progress we have and we are making.

Ladies and gentlemen, the costs now have been high. As we have lost our loved ones in this struggle, so have you. As we have mourned, so have you. This is a bitter price of combating tyranny and terror. Our hearts go to the families--every American who has given his or her life in the cause and every American who has been wounded to help us in our struggle. Now we are determined to honor your confidence and sacrifice by putting into practice in Iraq the values of liberty and democracy which are so dear to you, and which have triumphed over tyranny across our world.

Creating a democratic, prosperous, and stable nation where differences are respected, human rights protected, and which lives in peace with itself and its neighbors is our highest priority, our sternest challenge, and our greatest goal. It is a vision, I assure you, shared by the vast majority of the Iraqi people. But there are the tiny minority who despise the very ideas of liberty, of peace, of tolerance, and who will kill anyone, destroy anything to prevent Iraq and its people from achieving this goal. Among them are those who nurse fantasies of the former regime returning to power; there are fanatics who seek to impose a perverted vision of Islam in which the face of Allah cannot be seen; and there are terrorists, including many from outside Iraq, who seek to make our country the main battleground against freedom, democracy, and civilization. For the struggle in Iraq today is not about the future of Iraq only, it's about the worldwide war between those who want to live in peace and freedom, and terrorists, terrorists who strike indiscriminately at soldiers, at civilians, as they did so tragically on 9/11 in America, and as they did in Spain and Indonesia, Saudi Arabia, Turkey, Russia and my country and many others.

So in Iraq we confront both (an) insurgency and the global war on terror, with their destructive forces sometimes overlapping. These killers may be just a tiny fraction of our 27 million population, but with their guns and their suicide bombs to intimidate and to frighten all the people of Iraq, I can tell you today they will not succeed. For these murderers have no political program or cause other than (to) push our country back into tyranny. Their agenda is no different than terrorist forces that have struck all over the world, including in your own country on September 11th.

There lies the fatal weakness. The insurgency in Iraq is disruptive but small, and it has not and will never resonate with the Iraqi people. Iraqi citizens know better than anyone the horrors of dictatorship. This is (a) past we will never revisit.

Ladies and gentlemen, let me turn now to our plan which we have developed to meet the real challenges which Iraq faces today, a plan that we are successfully implementing with your help. The plan has three basic parts: building democracy, defeating the insurgency, and improving the quality of ordinary Iraqis' (lives.) The political strategy in our plan is to isolate the terrorists from the communities in which they operate. We are working hard to involve as many people as we can in the political process to cut the ground from under the terrorists' feet. In troubled areas across the country, government representatives are meeting with local leaders. They are offering amnesty to those who realize the error of their ways. They are making clear that there can be no compromise with terror, that all Iraqis have the opportunity to join the side of order and democracy, and that they should use the political process to address their legitimate concerns and hopes.

I am a realist; I know that terrorism cannot be defeated with political tools only. But we can weaken it, ending local support; (helping) us to tackle the enemy head-on to identify, isolate, and eradicate this cancer. Let me provide you with a couple of examples where this political plan already is working. In Samarra, the Iraqi government has tackled the insurgents who once controlled the city. Following weeks of discussions between government officials and representatives, coalition forces, and local community leaders, regular access to the city has been restored, a new provincial council and governor have been selected, and a new chief of police has been appointed. Hundreds of insurgents have been pushed out of the city by local citizens eager to get on with their lives. Today in Samarra, Iraqi forces are patrolling the city in close coordination with the coalition counterparts.

In Tall Afar, a city northwest of Baghdad, the Iraqi government has reversed an effort by insurgents to wrest control away from the proper authority. Iraqi forces put down the challenge and allowed local citizens to choose a new mayor and police chief. Thousands of civilians have returned to the city, and since their return, we have launched a large program of reconstruction and humanitarian assistance.

Ladies and gentlemen, let me turn now to our military strategy. We plan to build and maintain security forces across Iraq. Ordinary Iraqis are anxious to take over entirely this role and to shoulder all the security burdens of our country, as quickly as possible. For now, of course, we need the help of our American and coalition partners, but the training of Iraqi security forces is moving forward briskly and effectively. The Iraqi government now commands almost 50,000 armed and combat-ready Iraqis. By January it will be some 145,000 and by the end of next year some 250,000 Iraqis. The government has accelerated the development of Iraqi Special Forces and the establishment of a counterterrorist strike force, specific--to tackle specific problems posed by insurgencies.

Our intelligence is getting better every day. You have seen that--the successful resolution of the Najaf crisis and in the targeted attacks against insurgents in Fallujah. These new Iraqi forces are rising to a challenge. They are fighting on behalf of sovereign Iraqi government, and their performance is improving every day. Working closely with the coalition and other allies, they are striking their enemies wherever they hide, disrupting operations, destroying safe houses, and removing terrorist leaders.

But improving the everyday lives of Iraqis, tackling our economic problems is also essential to our plan. Across the country there is a daily progress too. Oil pipelines are being repaired, basic services are being improved, the homes are being rebuilt, schools and hospitals are being rebuilt, the clinics are open and reopened. There are now over 6 million children at school, many of them attending one of the 2,500 schools that have been renovated since liberation. Last week we completed a national polio vaccination campaign, reaching over 90 percent of all Iraqi children. We're starting work on 150 new health centers across the country. Millions of dollars in economic aid and humanitarian assistance from this country and others around the world are flowing into Iraq. For this, again, I want to thank you.

And so today, despite the setbacks and daily outrages, we can and should be hopeful for the future. In Najaf and Kufa, this plan has already brought success. In those cities, a firebrand cleric had taken over Shi'a Islam's holiest sites in defiance of the government and the local population. Immediately, the Iraqi government ordered the Iraqi armed forces to action, to use military force to create conditions for political success. Together with the coalition partners, Iraqi forces cleaned out insurgents from everywhere in the city, capturing hundreds and killings many more. At the same time, the government worked with political leaders and with Ayatollah Sistani to find a peaceful solution to the occupation of the shrine. We were successful. The shrine was preserved, order was restored, and Najaf and Kufa were returned to their citizens. Today, the foreign media have lost interest and left, but millions of dollars in economic aid and humanitarian assistance are now flowing into the cities. Ordinary citizens are once again free to worship at these places.

As we move forward, the next major milestone will be holding of the free and fair national and local elections in January next. I know that some have speculated, even doubted, whether this date can be met. So let me be absolutely clear. Elections will occur in Iraq, on time in January, because Iraqis want elections on time. For the skeptics who do not understand the Iraqi people, they do not realize how decades of torture and repression feed our desire for freedom. At every step of the political process to date, the courage and resilience of the Iraqi people (have) proved the doubters wrong. They said we would miss (the) January deadline to pass the interim constitution. We proved them wrong. They warned that there could be no successful handover of sovereignty by the end of June. We proved them wrong. A sovereign Iraq--(the) Iraqi government took over control two days early. They doubted whether a national conference could be staged this August. We proved them wrong. Despite intimidation and violence, over 1,400 citizens--a quarter of them women--from all regions and from every ethnic, religious and political grouping in Iraq elected a national council. And I pledge to you today we will prove them wrong again over the elections.

Our independent electoral commission is working with the United Nations, the multinational force, and our own Iraqi security forces to make these elections a reality. In 15 out of 18 of our Iraqi provinces, we could hold elections tomorrow. Although this is not what we see in your media, that is a fact. Your government, our government, and the United Nations are all helping us, mobilizing the necessary resources to fund voter registration and information programs. We will establish up to 30,000 polling sites, 130,000 election workers, and all other complex aspects mounting a general election in a nation of 27 million before the end of January next.

We already know that terrorists and former regime elements will do all they can to disrupt these elections. There would be no greater success for the terrorists if we delay, and no greater blow when the elections take place, as they will, on schedule. The Iraqi elections may not be perfect, may not be the best elections that Iraq will ever hold. They will no doubt be an excuse for violence from those that despise liberty, as were the first elections in Sierra Leone, South Africa, or Indonesia. But they will take place, and they will be free and fair. And though they won't be the end of the journey toward democracy, they will be a giant step forward in Iraq's political evolution. They will pave the way for a government that reflects the will and has the confidence of the Iraqi people.

Ladies and gentlemen, this is our strategy for moving Iraq steadily towards the security and democracy and prosperity our people crave. But Iraq cannot accomplish this alone. The resolve and will of the coalition in supporting a free Iraq is vital to our success. The Iraqi government needs the help of the international community, the help of countries that not only believe in the Iraqi people but also believe in the fight for freedom and against tyranny and terrorism everywhere. Already Iraq has many partners. The transition in Iraq from brutal dictatorship to freedom and democracy is not only an Iraqi endeavor; it is an international one. More than 30 countries are represented in Iraq with troops on the ground in harm's way. We Iraqis are grateful for each and every one of these courageous men and women. United Nations Resolution 1546, passed in June 2004, endorsed the Iraqi interim government and pledged international support for Iraq's upcoming elections. The G-8, the European Union and NATO have also issued formal statements of support. NATO is now helping with one of Iraq's most urgent needs, the training of Iraqi security forces. I am delighted by the new agreement to step up the pace and scope of this training.

The United Nations has reestablished its mission in Iraq, a new United Nations special representative has been appointed, and a team of United Nations personnel is now operating in Baghdad. Many more nations have committed to Iraq's future, in the form of economic aid. We

Iraqis are aware how international this effort truly is. But our opponents, the terrorists, also understand all too well that this is an international effort, and that's why they have targeted members of the coalition. I know the pain this causes. I know it is difficult, but the coalition must stand firm. When governments negotiate with terrorists, everyone in the free world suffers. When political leaders sound the siren of defeatism in the face of terrorism, it only encourages more violence. Working together, we will defeat the killers, and we will do this by refusing to bargain about our most fundamental principles.

Ladies and gentlemen, goodwill aside, I know that many observers around the world honestly wonder if we in Iraq really can restore our economy, be good neighbors, guarantee the democratic rule of law, and overcome the enemies who seek to tear us down. I understand why, faced with the daily headlines, there are these doubts. I know, too, that there will be many more setbacks and obstacles to overcome. But these doubters risk underestimating our country, and they risk fueling the hopes of the terrorists. Despite our problems, despite our recent history, no one should doubt that Iraq is a country of tremendous human resources and natural resources. Iraq is still a nation with an inspiring culture and a tradition, and an educated and civilized people. And Iraq is still a land made strong by its Islamic faith, which teaches us tolerance, love, respect and duty.

Above all, they risk underestimating the courage, determination of the Iraqi people to embrace democracy, peace and freedom, for the dreams of our families are the same as the dreams of the families here in America and around the world. There are those who want to divide our world. I appeal to you, who have done so much already to help us, to ensure they don't succeed. Do not allow them to say to Iraqis, to Arabs, to Muslims, that we have only two models of government--brutal dictatorship and religious extremism. This is wrong.

Like Americans, we Iraqis want to enjoy the fruits of liberty. Half of the world's 1.5 billion Muslims already enjoy democratically elected governments. As Prime Minister Blair said to you last year when he stood here, anywhere, anytime ordinary people are given the chance to choose, the choice is the same: Freedom not tyranny; democracy not dictatorship; and the rule of law, not the rule of the secret police. Do not let them convince others that the values of freedom, of tolerance and democracy are for you and the West but not for us.

For the first time in our history, the Iraqi people can look forward to controlling our own destiny. This would not have been possible without the help and sacrifices of this country and its coalition partners. I thank you again from the bottom of my heart. And let me tell you that as we meet, our greatest challenge, by building a democratic future, we the people of the new Iraq will remember those who have stood by us. As generous as you have been, we will stand with you too. As stalwart as you have been, we will stand with you too.

Neither tyranny nor terrorism has a place in our region or our world. And that is why we Iraqis will stand by you, America, in a war larger than either of our nations, the global battle to live in freedom. God bless you, and thank you.

THE AMERICAN CHARACTER

Character, in the long run, is the decisive factor
in the life of an individual and of nations alike.
--Theodore Roosevelt

What is the American Character? We can all name many people who embody it in one way or another. The leadership of George Washington, James Monroe, Theodore Roosevelt, or George S. Patton; the intrepidness of Daniel Boone, John Fremont, or Meriwether Lewis and William Clark; the courageous perseverance of Paul Revere, Harriet Tubman, or Helen Keller; the dignified brashness of Nathan Hale, Dred Scott, or Rosa Parks; the ingenuity of Thomas Edison, Benjamin Franklin, Jonas Salk, the Wright Brothers, or Walt Disney.

Often life's most difficult moments bring forth palpable representations of the American Character. It manifested itself in Dolly Madison's quick-thinking actions that saved national artistic treasures during the burning of the White House. In Francis Scott Key's composed temerity that enabled him to pen the lyrics to *The Star Spangled Banner* during the British siege of Fort McHenry. In Clara Barton's untiring frontline ministrations to wounded soldiers during numerous Civil War battles. In Dorie Miller's tenacious response to evil at Pearl Harbor. In J. Edgar Hoover's unflinching opposition to the internment of Japanese citizens during World War II. And in Ronald Reagan's graceful wit despite the pain of a would-be-assassin's bullet.

Still, these celebrated citizens represent merely the tip of the iceberg in terms of defining the American Character. When the Founding Fathers established a nation unlike any other ever known on earth, they laid a groundwork that fostered, nourished, and some would even say mandated a special type of persona. While individualism is a benchmark of Americans certain characteristics recur regularly--perseverance, optimism, dedication, valor, altruism, integrity, etc. These qualities are not exclusively American, yet they seem to thrive especially well among our populace. Inexplicably, they are found as abundantly among all class levels and appear as routinely in immigrants as they do in native born citizens.

Countless ordinary citizens demonstrate the American Character daily through quiet deeds. Names of individual Soldiers, Sailors, Airmen, Marines, and Coast Guard Personnel are usually only known to loved ones but their selfless sacrifices are felt by all. Few people know the name of the Boy Scout leaders who after a long day at the office still make every meeting. Only those in the gravest need get to meet the Salvation Army volunteers who seem to appear mysteriously within seconds of any disaster, but these anonymous souls personify the American Character. It is also daily displayed in the unsung actions of loyal spouses, loving parents, heroic policemen and firemen, honest merchants, ethical businessmen, caring doctors and nurses, committed teachers, reverent clergy, wholesome performers, and all who strive to do what is right even when it is not the easy choice.

Some have earned renown for boldly displaying the American Character, but millions more will never seek nor achieve fame by living its virtues daily. It is the vigorous adherence to such lofty ideals by so many Americans of Character that ensures the United States will remain the Shining City on a Hill.

No arsenal or no weapon in the arsenals of the world is so formidable as the will and moral courage of free men and women.--Ronald Reagan

Great necessities call out great virtues.--Abigail Adams

While people elsewhere operated on the premise, 'If I haven't got it, he shouldn't have it either, Americans seemed to say, "If he's got it, I ought to be able to have it too, if I just work hard enough."--Balint Vazsonyi[1]--

We must accept finite disappointment, but never lose infinite hope.--Martin Luther King, Jr.

My toast would be, may our country always be successful, but whether successful or otherwise, always right.--John Quincy Adams

I never did anything worth doing by accident, nor did any of my inventions come by accident; they came by work.--Thomas Edison

To sin by silence when they should protest makes cowards of men.--Abraham Lincoln

Let the word go forth from this time and place, to friend and foe alike, that the torch has been passed to a new generation of Americans--born in this century, tempered by war, disciplined by a hard and bitter peace.--John Kennedy

Optimism is the faith that leads to achievement. Nothing can be done without hope and confidence.--Helen Keller

The man who can look upon a crisis without being willing to offer himself upon the altar of his country is not fit for public trust.--Millard Fillmore

Progress occurs when courageous, skillful leaders seize the opportunity to change things for the better.--Harry Truman

The credit belongs to the man who is actually in the arena, whose face is marred by dust and sweat and blood; who strives valiantly; who errs and comes up short again and again, who knows the great enthusiasms, the great devotions, and spends himself in a worthy cause; who at best, knows the triumph of high achievement; and who, at the worst, if he fails, at least fails while daring greatly, so that his place shall never be with those cold and timid souls who know neither victory nor defeat. --Theodore Roosevelt

I am confident about the future of America. I believe in you. I know that the future of our country, our culture, and our children is in good hands. I know you will continue to meet adversity with strength and resilience as our ancestors did, and come through with flying colors--the ones on Old Glory.--Charlton Heston

More and more we need understanding and appreciation of those principles upon which the republic was founded. What were those 'self-evident' truths that so many risked all for, fought for, suffered and died for? What was the source of their courage? Who were those people? I don't think we can ever know enough about them.--David McCullough[2]

Too many of us look upon Americans as dollar chasers. This is a cruel libel, even if it is reiterated thoughtlessly by the Americans themselves.--Albert Einstein

Patriotism is not a short and frenzied outburst of emotion but the tranquil and steady dedication of a lifetime.-- Adlai Stevenson

Honor lies in honest toil.--Grover Cleveland

Nearly all men can stand adversity, but if you want to test a man's character, give him power.--Abraham Lincoln

In no other land could a boy from a country village, without inheritance or influential friends, look forward with unbounded hope.--Herbert Hoover

These astronauts knew the dangers and they faced them willingly, knowing they had a high and noble purpose in life. Because of their courage and daring and idealism, we will miss them all the more.--George W. Bush on Columbia's crew

They made the ultimate sacrifice, giving their lives in service to their country and for all mankind. Their dedication and devotion to the exploration of space was an inspiration to each of us and still motivates people around the world to achieve great things in service to others.--Columbia Commander Rick Husband on the 17th anniversary of Challenger's tragedy 4 days before his flight's tragedy.[3]

Man is an artifact designed for space travel. He is not designed to remain in his present biologic state any more than a tadpole is designed to remain a tadpole.--William S. Burroughs

You gain strength, courage and confidence by every experience in which you really stop to look fear in the face. --Eleanor Roosevelt

There is nothing wrong with America that Americans can't fix. --Ronald Reagan

Character cannot be developed in ease and quiet. Only through experience of trial and suffering can the soul be strengthened, ambition inspired, and success achieved.--Helen Keller

When you can do the common things in life in an uncommon way, you will command the attention of the world.--George Washington Carver

Courage is fear holding on a minute longer.--George S. Patton

Courage and perseverance have a magical talisman, before which difficulties disappear and obstacles vanish into air. --John Quincy Adams

We are not weak, if we make proper use of those means which the God of nature hath placed in our power.--Patrick Henry

Wealth can only be accumulated by the earnings of industry and the savings of frugality.--John Tyler

Life is not easy, and least of all is it easy for either the man or the nation that aspires to great deeds.--Theodore Roosevelt

Character is power.--Booker T. Washington

Cowardice asks the question, "Is it safe?" Expediency asks the question, "Is it politic?" Vanity asks the question, "Is it popular?" But, conscience asks the question, "Is it right?" And there comes a time when one must take a position that is neither safe, nor politic, nor popular, but one must take it because one's conscience tells one that it is right.--Martin Luther King, Jr.

Fame is a vapor, popularity an accident, and riches take wings. Only one thing endures and that is character.--Horace Greeley

The men who succeed the best in public life are those who take the risk of standing by their own convictions.--James Garfield

The courage of life is often a less dramatic spectacle than the courage of the final moment; but it is no less a magnificent mixture of triumph and tragedy.--John F. Kennedy

The hero is one who kindles a great light in the world, who sets up blazing torches in the dark streets of life for men to see by. --Felix Adler

I'd rather give my life than be afraid to give it.--Lyndon Johnson

God chooses righteous men and nations to act as the agents of righteousness and blessing. The United States, despite its imperfections, is by far one of the most moral, praiseworthy countries in the world. Perhaps this is why it was Divinely granted the power and means to fight evil and create a better world.--Yaffa Ganz

Don't expect to build up the weak by pulling down the strong. --Calvin Coolidge

We have to do with the past only as we can make it useful to the present and the future.--Frederick Douglass

In any moment of decision the best thing you can do is the right thing, the next best thing is the wrong thing and the worst thing you can do is nothing.--Theodore Roosevelt

My affections were first for my own country and then generally for all mankind.--Thomas Jefferson

I know in my heart and my brain that America ain't what's wrong in the world.--Donald Rumsfeld

America isn't great because of what government did for the people. America is great because free people have had the chance and the incentive and the opportunity to dream, strive and work toward their goals. That's what has made America great.--Ronald Reagan

Alone we can do so little, together we can do so much. --Helen Keller

One of my superstitions had always been when I started to go anywhere, or to do anything, not to turn back, or stop until the thing intended was accomplished.--Ulysses S. Grant

Be always sure you're right, then go ahead.--Davy Crockett

I sought for the greatness and genius of America in her commodious harbors and her ample rivers, and it was not there; in the fertile fields and boundless prairies, and it was not there; in her rich mines and her vast world commerce, and it was not there. Not until I went into the churches of America and heard her pulpits aflame with righteousness did I understand the secret of her genius and power. America is great because America is good--and if America ever ceases to be good--America will cease to be great.--Alexis de Tocqueville

I want it said of me by those who knew me best, that I always plucked a thistle and planted a flower where I thought a flower would grow.--Abraham Lincoln

It is hard to fail, but it is worse never to have tried to succeed. --Theodore Roosevelt

The spirit of Lincoln still lives; that spirit born of the teachings of the Nazarene, who promised mercy to the merciful, who lifted the lowly, strengthened the weak, ate with publicans, and made the captives free. In the light of this divine example, the doctrines of demagogues shiver in their chaff. --Martin Luther King, Jr.

Those who are really in earnest are willing to be anything or nothing in the world's estimation, and publicly and privately, in season and out, avow their sympathies with despised ideas and their advocates, and bear the consequences.--Susan B. Anthony

It's not what they take away from you that counts. It's what you do with what you have left.--Hubert Humphrey

Double--no triple--our troubles and we'd still be better off than any other people on earth.--Ronald Reagan

One must think like a hero to behave like a merely decent human being.--May Sarton

90

Let us endeavor so to live that when we come to die even the undertaker will be sorry.--Mark Twain

Labor disgraces no man, but occasionally men disgrace labor.
--Ulysses S. Grant

Associate yourself with men of good quality if you esteem your own reputation. It is better be alone than in bad company.
--George Washington

I think there is only one quality worse than hardness of heart and that is softness of head.--Theodore Roosevelt

Accept the challenges so you can feel the exhilaration of victory.
--George S. Patton

Moral courage is a more rare commodity than bravery in battle or great intelligence.--Robert Kennedy

Excellence is to do a common thing in an uncommon way.
--Booker T. Washington

Americans have the appealing if self-defeating habit of projecting their values onto others who haven't enjoyed centuries of self-enlightenment. But we learn and mean well.--Kathleen Parker[4]

America is a fabulously wealthy and unbelievably strong nation. It can lose many material things and still survive. What it cannot lose and expect to survive as a nation is its national character. And if America's leadership loses its character, rooted in morality, the rest will of necessity follow.--John L. Perry[5]

Rules cannot substitute for character.--Alan Greenspan

If you haven't got any charity in your heart, you have the worst kind of heart trouble.--Bob Hope

If passion drives you, let reason hold the reins.
--Benjamin Franklin

I don't think I did anything for this country--the American people decided it was time to right the ship, and I was just the captain they put on the bridge when they did it.--Ronald Reagan

To love your country is a wonderful thing. To love your country, to love God, to love family. It motivates me and fills my heart, and I don't think it's bad.--Claudia Bermudez

Americanism is a question of principles, of idealism, of character: it is not a matter of birthplace or creed or line of descent.--Theodore Roosevelt

If a man is called to be a street sweeper, he should sweep streets even as Michelangelo painted, or Beethoven composed music or Shakespeare wrote poetry. He should sweep streets so well that all the hosts of heaven and earth will pause to say, here lived a great street sweeper who did his job well.--Martin Luther King, Jr.

No pessimist ever discovered the secret of the stars or sailed to an uncharted land or opened a new heaven to the human spirit.
--Helen Keller

I do the very best I know how, the very best I can, and I mean to keep doing so until the end.--Abraham Lincoln

There is little use for the being whose tepid soul knows nothing of the great and generous emotion, of the high pride, the stern belief, the lofty enthusiasm, of the men who quell the storm and ride the thunder.--Theodore Roosevelt

Stand upright, speak thy thoughts, declare the truth thou hast, that all may share; Be bold, proclaim it everywhere: They only live who dare.--Lewis Morris

Elihu Root was a statesman who gained renown through his exemplification of the American Character. By admirably serving as Secretary of Defense (then called Secretary of War) under William McKinley and Secretary of State under Theodore Roosevelt and later as a senator from New York, he followed in the footsteps of many great Americans whose legacies still inspire millions. In the dissertation below he astutely expounded on the essence of one public servant who profoundly influenced the lives of all who came after him. Abraham Lincoln is the one American of Character we should all strive to emulate. Secretary Root who was born in 1845 had a fresher perspective on Lincoln than modern historians, but the sober judgment of time was already starting to grasp the sixteenth president's greatness. As this probing appraisal clearly demonstrates, Secretary Root thoroughly comprehended his subject's contributions and appropriately appreciated Abraham Lincoln's probity. This address was first published in 1924.

Lincoln as a Leader Of Men
by Elihu Root

The life of Abraham Lincoln is full of appeals to the imagination; its dramatic quality absorbs attention. The humble beginnings, the early poverty, the slender opportunity for even the simplest education, the swift rise from the ordinary lot to the heights of station and of power, the singular absence of those aids by which personal ambition commonly seeks its ends, the transcendent moral quality of the cause which he came to lead, the desperate struggle, the triumphant success, the tragic ending, the startling contrast between the abuse and ridicule to which he was so long subjected, and the honor and glory for all time which he achieved--all these tend completely to fill the minds of those who read or listen to the story of Lincoln.

There is another view of Lincoln's life, however, which we

ought not to overlook, and from which a useful lesson may be learned. He was intensely practical. While he never for a moment lost sight of the great ends toward which he struggled, or wavered in his devotion to the eternal principles which justified those ends, he never assumed that his conclusions would be accepted merely because he knew they were right, however clearly he might state them. He did not expect other people to have their minds work as his mind worked, or to reach his conclusions because he thought they ought to reach them, or to feel as he felt because he thought they ought to feel so. He never relied upon authority or dictation or compulsion upon the minds of others.

Never concealing or obscuring his ideals, avowing them, declaring them, constant to them, setting them high for guidance as if among the stars, he kept his feet on the earth, he minded his steps, he studied the country to be traversed, its obstacles, its possible aids to progress. He studied the material with which he had to work--the infinite varieties of human nature, the good, the bad, and, predominantly, the indifferent; the widely differing material interests of sections and of occupations; the inherited traditions and prejudices, the passions and weaknesses, sympathies and dislikes, the ignorance and misunderstanding, the successive stages of slowly developing opinion, the selfishness and the altruism. He understood that to lead a nation in emergency he had to bring all these forces into such relations to his design and to each other that the resultant of forces would be in the direction of his purpose.

This was the field of Lincoln's great struggle, and here he won by infinite patience and sagacity. During those terrible years of the Rebellion he was not disturbing himself about what principles he ought to maintain or what end he ought to seek. He was struggling with the weaknesses and perversities of human nature at home. He was smoothing away obstacles and converting enemies and strengthening friends, and bending all possible motives and desires and prejudices into the direction of his steady purpose. Many people thought, while he was doing this, that he was trifling, that he was yielding where he ought to have been splendidly courageous and peremptory. He understood as they did not how to bend his material without breaking it; he understood as they did not how many a jest bridged over a difficult situation, and made it possible to avoid a quarrel injurious to the Union cause.

Lincoln's whole life had been a training for just this kind of struggle. He had begun at the bottom, in a community of simple, poor, and for the most part uneducated people, and he had learned in his contests for the State Legislature to win the support of those people by actual personal contact and influence, standing absolutely on a level with them, and without any possible assumption of superiority or right of dictation. He had moved along up the scale of association with people of broader minds and greater education and more trained intelligence, developing himself as he moved on, but never changing his method of winning agreement. This was always by a frank and honest declaration of principle and purpose, accompanied by the most skillful and sympathetic appeal to the human nature of the man with whom he dealt; based upon a careful study of the capacities and prejudices and motives of that man.

He had three qualities of the highest value. The first was sympathy--genuine appreciative sympathy for all his fellow men. Contemplation of human nature furnishes nothing more encouraging than the general response of mankind to such a quality; it cannot be simulated; it must be real; and then it begets its like in others. Secretary Stanton used to get out of patience with Lincoln because he was all the time pardoning men who ought to be shot; but no one can tell how much the knowledge of that quality in him drew the people of the country toward him and won their confidence and support. Above all, that quality enabled him to understand men, to appreciate how they felt, and why they acted as they did, and how they could be set right when they were wrong.

The second quality was a sense of proportion, with which is always associated humor, or a sense of humor. He knew intuitively what was big and important and must be insisted upon, and what might seem big, but was really small and unimportant, and might be sacrificed without harm. Such a statement may seem a matter of course and of little consequence; but, if we look back in history, we can see that a large part of the most bitter controversies in politics and religion and statecraft and opinion in all fields have been about matters which really were not in themselves of the slightest consequence; and we may realize how important it is in great crises to have leaders who can form the same kind of judgment about the relative importance of questions at issue that future generations may readily form in the reading of history.

The third quality of Lincoln's was his subordination of himself to his cause. He liked to get on in the world, of course, as any normal man does; but the way he got on was by thinking about his job, not by thinking about himself. During all these years he was not thinking about making Abraham Lincoln famous; he was thinking about putting an end to slavery and preserving the Union. It is interesting to observe that the two who have attained the highest pinnacles are not to be found among the millions of Americans who have dreamed of power and fame for themselves. (George) Washington and Lincoln reached their preeminence by thinking about their work and forgetting themselves.

Lincoln never made the mistake of using words--either oral or written--merely for his own satisfaction. Many fine sentiments are uttered about public affairs, which are not really designed to have an effect upon anybody except the speaker or writer whose feelings are gratified by expression. They are like the use of expletives--profane and otherwise--which simply relieve the feelings of the speaker. Lincoln never made this mistake. When he spoke or wrote, his objective was always the mind of somebody else.

His method with individuals is well illustrated by the incident when a committee of gentlemen called upon him to object to the use of Negro troops. They said they were all patriotic citizens, that their sons were serving in the Union Army, and were cultivated gentlemen, and they objected to having Negroes put upon the same level. Mr. Lincoln said: "Well, gentlemen, if you would rather have your sons die for a black man than have a black man die for your sons, I suppose there is nothing more to be said." This was a wholly new view of the subject. The objectors were prepared to stand for all time against arguments designed to force them to abandon their prejudice. Lincoln, however, had instantly found the line of least resistance, which left the prejudice undisturbed and at the same time left them nothing to say; so the objection ended.

Another illustration on a broader field is to be found in the great debates with (Stephen) Douglas. From first to last, in these debates, he insisted upon the fundamental proposition that slavery was morally wrong and ought not to continue. He knew, however, that the conservatism and the material interests and the unawakened conscience of the North could not then be arrayed in favor of destroying slavery in the slave states at the expense of destroying the Constitution.

Accordingly, he carefully and consistently disclaimed any such proposal, and limited himself to demanding that slavery should be restricted to the states where it already existed under the protection of the Constitution, and that its extension should be prevented just as it had been prevented by the ordinance for the Government of the Northwest Territory in 1787, in confidence that, if restricted, it would die a natural death, just as the framers of the Constitution believed it would die when they agreed to the compromises of the Constitution. Upon that proposition, to prevent the extension of slavery because slavery was wrong, he enlisted the public opinion of the North and made possible the election of a Republican President in 1860. In the struggle of the South against that proposition a new situation was created, and in 1863 the whole North accepted the complete emancipation upon which they would have divided fatally five years before.

The Emancipation Proclamation itself illustrates the same wise solicitude to keep the people upon whose support he relied close behind his leadership. After declaring that the slaves shall be free, he concludes with the following paragraph: "And upon this act, sincerely believed to be an act of justice warranted by the Constitution upon military necessity, I invoke the considerate judgment of mankind and the gracious favor of Almighty God."

It would be difficult to conceive of a broader appeal to more varied kinds of men and phases of opinion than is contained in this single sentence of thirty-three words. It commands the interest and conciliates the support of all who love justice, of all who revere the Constitution, of all who are determined that the sacrifices of the country in the war shall not have been in vain, of all who regard the judgment of mankind, of all whose sympathy is enlisted by action reverent in spirit and seeking for Divine guidance. It claims no credit for Abraham Lincoln but it places the great act, with a fitting sense of proportion, on a basis to command universal approval and support.

One of the most valuable results of Lincoln's training was that he understood the necessity of political organization for the accomplishment of political ends. He knew that to attain a great public purpose multitudes of men must be induced to lay aside or postpone or in some way subordinate their minor differences of opinion, and to move together on the lines of major policy. He used all the resources of party organization to hold the people of the North to the support of the Northern armies in the field. Lincoln was a politician, the best practical politician of his time. If he had not been that, the Northern armies would have been abandoned; the Union would have been broken, to the infinite injury of both sections; and slavery would have continued, no one knows how long--probably until another war had been fought.

It will be useful to remember that Abraham Lincoln was a politician. The word is often used as a term of reproach. Such a use indicates the most superficial thinking, or, rather, failure to think. To be a corrupt and self seeking politician ought of course to be a reproach, just as it is a discredit to be a corrupt or unfair businessman. Politics is the practical exercise of the art of self-government, and somebody must attend to it if we are to have self-government; somebody must study it, and learn the art, and exercise patience and sympathy and skill to bring the multitude of opinions and wishes of self-governing people into such order that some prevailing opinion may be expressed and peaceably accepted. Otherwise, confusion will result either in dictatorship or anarchy.

The principal ground of reproach against any American citizen should be that he is not a politician. Everyone ought to be, as Lincoln was.

AMERICAN CULTURE

I am certain that after the dust of centuries
has passed over our cities, we, too, will be
remembered not for victories or defeats in
battle or in politics, but for our contribution
to the human spirit.--John F. Kennedy

Like the American Character, the nation's Culture is hard to
describe, but it is easy to spot. It is more than the enthralling fiction of
Herman Melville, Nathaniel Hawthorne, F. Scott Fitzgerald, Louis
L'amour, and Harold Bell Wright; broader than the stirring poetry of
Anne Bradstreet, William Wadsworth Longfellow, Emily Dickinson
and Walt Whitman. It proudly includes the masterful sculptures of
John Gutzon Borglum, Edward Kemeys, and Robert Tait McKenzieor
and inspired paintings of James Whistler and Andrew Wyeth. It
incorporates the musical geniuses of many genres. George and Ira
Gershwin brought Edna Ferber's epic novel *Show Boat* to the stage
and gave birth to the American Musical. George M. Cohan, Jerome
Kern, Alan Jay Lerner and Frederick Loewe, and Irving Berlin
ensured that it lives a rousing life. Duke Ellington and Louis
Armstrong escorted jazz into the mainstream. Jimmie Rodgers and
Hank Williams laid a secure foundation for Country Music; Bill
Monroe spun off its cousin Bluegrass. Carl Perkins, Elvis Presley and
Johnny Cash gave us rockabilly. Hollywood has certainly turned out
its share of duds that shame us but the Silver Screen has also elevated
American culture with *Gone With the Wind, Casablanca, The Sound
of Music, Star Wars, Rain Man,* and many other salubrious titles.
Former Federal Communications Commission Chairman Newton
Minow rightly termed Television a vast wasteland but that annoying
little box in our living rooms has made generations laugh thanks to the
wit of Lucille Ball, Bob Hope, Jack Benny, and Johnny Carson.

Still the American culture encompasses much more than its artistic accomplishments. It includes Southern hospitality and California's wine country. New England accents and the Rocky Mountains. The Lincoln Memorial and Yellowstone National Park, The Tournament of Roses Parade and The Empire State Building. The Golden Gate Bridge and the St. Louis Arch. The Super Bowl and the World Series. Rush hour traffic and shopping malls. *Jeopardy* and Trivial Pursuit. Philadelphia cheese steaks and Louisiana cajun delights. The Astrodome and the Grand Canyon. Bugs Bunny and *the Saturday Evening Post. Reader's Digest* and the Grand Old Opry. Talk radio and Thanksgiving dinner. Little league games and Fourth of July cookouts. It's volunteering for community projects and helping our neighbors, It's supporting our troops and doing our part!

But its even more than the sum of all these things too, and that's why any definition would ultimately prove inchoate. The American culture has as many components as there are Americans. Every aspect exists solely because of the efforts of individual Americans--no two of us would likely explain it the same way, but united we produce a very powerful and readily discernable ethos.

The eclectic quotes in this section do not revolve around a tangible common theme, but together they appropriately limn the American culture.

America lives in the heart of every man everywhere who wishes to find a region where he will be free to work out his destiny as he chooses. --Woodrow Wilson

Freedom and dignity of the individual have been more assured here than any other place on earth.--Ronald Reagan

There has never yet been a man in our history who led a life of ease whose name is worth remembering.--Theodore Roosevelt

While American soldiers are dying overseas to protect our freedom, we're becoming slaves to malevolence in our own homes. While we're subjected to body searches at airports, increased monitoring of communications, and constantly changing terror alerts – all to combat terrorists who would destroy our nation – we invite cultural terrorists into our homes and allow them to destroy our sensibilities and the innocence of our children.--Rebecca Hagelin[1]

Is this a great country or what?--Charlie Daniels

Courage and grace is a formidable mixture.--Marlene Dietrich

Hollywood has failed miserably in broadcasting to the rest of the world the truth about America's fundamental kindness, decency, generosity, patriotism and deep religious faith--all traits abundantly displayed in the days since September 11.--Michael Medved[2]

I'm proud to be paying taxes in the United States. The only thing is--I could be just as proud for half the money.--Arthur Godfrey

Our American values are not luxuries, but necessities--not the salt in our bread, but the bread itself.--Jimmy Carter

A long habit of not thinking a thing wrong, gives it a superficial appearance of being right.--Thomas Paine

Popularity, I have always thought, may aptly be compared to a coquette, the more you woo her, the more apt is she to elude your embrace. --John Tyler

We can't all be heroes because someone has to sit on the curb and clap as they go by.--Will Rogers

The millions of Americans who live decent, praiseworthy lives deserve our highest admiration because they have opted for the good when the good is not the only available option.--Dinesh D'Souza[3]

Let my name stand among those who are willing to bear ridicule and reproach for the truth's sake, and so earn some right to rejoice when the victory is won.--Louisa May Alcott

Capitalism is merely human freedom applied to economics.--Lowell Ponte[4]

It's only the horrible that needs to sneak up on us. Americans always let the wonderful in the front door.--Tammy Bruce[5]

Two things in America are astonishing: the changeableness of most human behavior and the strange stability of certain principles. Men are constantly on the move, but the spirit of humanity seems almost unmoved.--Alexis De Tocqueville

The trouble with this country is that there are too many people going about saying, "The trouble with this country is..."--Sinclair Lewis

Perhaps this is our strange and haunting paradox here in America--that we are fixed and certain only when we are in movement.--Thomas Wolfe

There is nothing wrong with America that faith, love of freedom, intelligence, and the energy of her citizens cannot cure.--Dwight D. Eisenhower

Somehow I can't believe that there are any heights that can't be scaled by a man who knows the secrets of making dreams come true.--Walt Disney

One cannot be an American by going about saying that one is an American. It is necessary to feel America, like America, love America and then work.--Georgia O'Keefe

The stealth bomber is supposed to be a big deal. It flies in undetected, bombs, then flies away. Hell, I've been doing that all my life.--Bob Hope

The ultimate economic and spiritual unit of any civilization is still the family.--Clare Booth Luce

The bravest things we do in our lives are usually known only to ourselves. No one throws ticker tape on the man who chose to be faithful to his wife, on the lawyer who didn't take the drug money, or the daughter who held her tongue again and again--all this anonymous heroism.--Peggy Noonan

If we keep treating our most important values as meaningless relics, that's exactly what they'll become.--Michael Josephson

It's not a question of live and let live, it's a question of right and wrong. --Archbishop Sean P. O'Malley

The capacity for harm is diminished because so many stood solidly behind America while we tried to bring it down. The country is stronger for having encountered and withstood us.--Ronald Radosh, an ex-communist[6]

Moderation in temper is always a virtue; but moderation in principle is always a vice.--Thomas Paine

What America has done for me could not have been done for me alone and could not have been done at all if the institutions, ideas, and attitudes that grew out of its founding assumption had not been in place and applicable to all who were lucky enough to live under them.--Norman Podhoretz[7]

The virtues of courage and patriotism have given recent proof of their continued presence and increasing power in the hearts and over the lives of our people. The influences of religion have been multiplied and strengthened. The sweet offices of charity have greatly increased. The virtue of temperance is held in higher estimation. We have not attained an ideal condition. Not all of our people are happy and prosperous; not all of them are virtuous and law-abiding. But on the whole the opportunities offered to the individual to secure the comforts of life are better than are found elsewhere and largely better than they were here one hundred years ago.--Benjamin Harrison

Americans are a tolerant lot, and we've put up with a lot of licentiousness, but most of us value self-restraint and self-reliance over self-indulgence and sensationalism. (Cable TV just hasn't yet got the message.) Most of us value family, faith, liberty, financial opportunity, fairness and responsibility. We take seriously the common core of ideas, the "self-evident truths" articulated by the Founding Fathers.--Suzanne Fields[8]

Fear is a disease that eats away at logic and makes man inhuman.
--Marian Anderson

There is no question that we have failed to live up to the dreams of the Founding Fathers many times and in many places. Sometimes we do better than others. But all in all, the one thing we must be on guard against is thinking that because of this, the system has failed. The system has not failed. Some human beings have failed the system.--Ronald Reagan

The noblest search is the search for excellence.--Lyndon Johnson

Nothing in the world is more dangerous than sincere ignorance and conscientious stupidity.--Martin Luther King, Jr.

In the beginning of a change, the Patriot is a scarce man--brave, hated, and scorned. When his cause succeeds however, the timid join him, for then it costs nothing to be a Patriot.--Mark Twain

In attempting to raise children without two parents, we are seeing on a massive scale, the voluntary breakup of the minimal family unit. This is historically unprecedented, an authentic cultural revolution and I believe socially calamitous.--William Bennett[9]

We have to depend on ourselves in this country right now because we can't depend on anyone else. We are simultaneously the most loved, hated, feared, and respected nation on this planet.--Dennis Miller

Life is 10 percent what you make it and 90 percent how you take it.
--Irving Berlin

The western spirit is, or will yet be (for no other is, or can be) the true American one.--Herman Melville

It's the quality of the ordinary, the straight, the square, that accounts for the great stability and success of our nation. It's a quality to be proud of. But it's a quality that many people seem to have neglected.--Gerald Ford

Regardless of the mushrooming numbers of people who call themselves artists, there are still very few who are working on a level that earns them the title *artist*.--Lynn Munson[10]*

Instead of finding a handful of prudes or religious zealots as pro-pornography forces are likely to dub those who try to tell the truth, I found liberals and conservatives, religious individuals and those who have turned away from God. I found rich and poor. I found children of CEOs of fortune 500 companies and children of ghetto families.--Tonya Flynt-Vega on anti-pornography activists[11]

It is not what we have that will make us a great nation; it is the way in which we use it.--Theodore Roosevelt

How vain it is to sit down to write when you have not stood up to live.
--Henry David Thoreau

The ultimate determinant in the struggle that's now going on in the world will not be bombs and rockets, but a test of wills and ideas, a trial of spiritual resolve, the values we hold, the beliefs we cherish, the ideals to which we are dedicated.--Ronald Reagan

The best way to get yourself a reputation as a dangerous citizen is to go about repeating the very phrases which our Founding Fathers used in the struggle for independence.--Charles Austin Beard

Some people call me an idealist. Well, that is the way I know I am an American. America is the only idealist nation in the world. --Woodrow Wilson

This nation can never be conquered from without. If it is ever to fall it will be from within.--Abraham Lincoln

For this is what America is all about. It is the uncrossed desert and the unclimbed ridge. It is the star that is not reached and the harvest that is sleeping in the unplowed ground.--Lyndon Johnson

Our country has been populated by pioneers, and therefore it has more energy, more enterprise, more expansive power than any other in the whole world.--Theodore Roosevelt

From the wild Irish slums of the 19th century eastern seaboard, to the riot-torn suburbs of Los Angeles, there is one unmistakable lesson in American history: A community that allows a large number of young men to grow up in broken families, dominated by women, never acquiring any stable relationship to male authority, never acquiring any rational expectations about the future--that community asks for and gets chaos. --Daniel Patrick Moynihan

A nation is formed by the willingness of each of us to share in the responsibility for upholding the common good.--Barbara Jordan

There are no easy answers, but there are simple answers.--Ronald Reagan

The ultimate measure of a man is not where he stands in moments of comfort and convenience, but where he stands at times of challenge and controversy.--Martin Luther King, Jr.

The highest patriotism is not a blind acceptance of official policy, but a love of one's country deep enough to call her to a higher standard.
--George McGovern

I'm liberal 99 percent of the time. I just want two things: to keep one of every two dollars I make, and to have the bad guys killed before they kill us.--Dennis Miller

We dare not forget that we are heirs of that first revolution.
--John F. Kennedy

The rule is perfect: in all matters of opinion our adversaries are insane.
--Mark Twain

"Adult bookstores"--the euphemism has it--as if there is something uniquely adult rather than pathetically juvenile about pornography.
--Gertrude Himmelfarb[12]

Pornography leaves a scar on the soul of anyone who embraces it.
--Kelly Boggs[13]

America's day begins with sunrise over Guam and the Northern Marianas, America's day ends when the sun sets over the western shore of the island of Tutuila in American Samoa.--Gale Norton

After industry and frugality, nothing contributes more to the raising of a young man in the world than punctuality and justice in his dealings.
--Benjamin Franklin

Another plague upon the land, as devastating as the locusts God loosed on the Egyptians, is "Political Correctness."--Charlton Heston

Quality means doing it right when no one is looking.--Henry Ford

If Hollywood refuses to support America, why should we support Hollywood?--Michele Malkin[14]

A hunch is creativity trying to tell you something.--Frank Capra

By profession I am a soldier and take great pride in that fact, but I am prouder, infinitely prouder, to be a father. A soldier destroys in order to build; the father only builds, never destroys. The one has the potentialities of death; the other embodies creations and life. And while the hordes of death are mighty, the battalions of life are mightier still.--Douglas MacArthur

I have never been lost, but I will admit to being confused for several weeks.--Daniel Boone

You may have a fresh start any moment you choose, for this thing that we call "Failure" is not the falling down, but the staying down.--Mary Pickford

There is nothing in the world of art like the songs mother used to sing. --Billy Sunday

It is impossible to win the race unless you venture to run, impossible to win the victory unless you dare to battle.--Richard DeVos

I sometimes think that the saving grace of America lies in the fact that the overwhelming majority of Americans are possessed of two great qualities- a sense of humor and a sense of proportion.--Franklin Delano Roosevelt

For other nations, utopia is a blessed past never to be recovered; for Americans it is just beyond the horizon.--Henry Kissinger

As difficult as the American culture is to explain, the impact it has on many is not hard to see. The ever-available expression of so many viewpoints cannot help but enlighten those with access to even a fraction of the offerings. Still, that may be one reason why it provokes so much animosity from evildoers. After September 11 some terrorist apologists blamed the baser elements of our culture--embarrassingly obtainable around the world--with instigating the anger of those whose cultures disavow such carnalities. The inherently weak argument loses all credibility when faced with the fact that most of the 9-11 terrorists spent their final nights indulging in acts of profuse decadence that their societies allegedly forbid.

As Chairman of the National Endowment of the Humanities Bruce Cole certainly has his finger on the pulse of America's culture. In this engrossing stemwinder delivered to National Citizen Corps Conference on July 29, 2003 he convincingly spelled out why our cultural milestones are vitally important and why our enemies hate them.

Remarks by NEH Chairman Bruce Cole
to the National Citizen Corps Conference

In his Inaugural Address, President Bush called on all Americans to be citizens, not spectators; to serve our nation, beginning with our neighbors; to speak for the values that gave our nation birth. That call took on new meaning after the attacks of September 11. We witnessed the true measure of what it is to be a good citizen--when evil is countered with acts of courage and compassion.

As chairman of the National Endowment for the Humanities (NEH), my duty is to share the wisdom of the humanities with all Americans. The humanities are, in short, the study of what makes us human: the legacy of our past, the ideas and principles that motivate us, and the eternal questions that we still ponder. The classics and archeology show us whence our civilization came. The study of literature and art shape our sense of beauty. The knowledge of philosophy and religion give meaning to our concepts of justice and goodness.

The NEH was founded in the belief that cultivating the best of the humanities has real, tangible benefits for civic life. Our founding legislation declares that "democracy demands wisdom." America must have educated and thoughtful citizens who can fully and intelligently participate in our government of, by and for the people. The NEH exists to foster the wisdom and knowledge essential to our national identity and survival.

Indeed, the state of the humanities has real implications for the state of our union. Our nation is in a conflict driven by religion, philosophy, political ideology and views of history--all humanities subjects. Our tolerance, our principles, our wealth and our liberties have made us targets. To understand this conflict, we need the humanities.

The values implicit in the study of the humanities are part of why we were attacked. The free and fearless exchange of ideas, respect for individual conscience, belief in the power of education--all these things are anathema to our country's enemies. Understanding and affirming these principles is part of the battle.

The attack on September 11 targeted not only innocent civilians, but also the very fabric of our culture. The terrorists struck the Twin Towers and the Pentagon and aimed at either the White House or Capitol dome--all structures rich in meaning and bearing witness to the United States' free commerce, military strength, and democratic government. As such, they also housed many of the artifacts--the manuscripts, art and archives--that form our history and heritage.

In the weeks following the attack, the NEH awarded a grant to an organization that conducted a survey of the damage to our cultural holdings. They found that the attack obliterated numerous art collections of great worth. Cantor Fitzgerald's renowned "museum in the sky" is lost, as well as priceless works by Rodin, Picasso, Hockney, Lichtenstein, Corbusier, Miro and others.

Archaeological artifacts from the African Burial Ground and other Manhattan sites are gone forever, as are irreplaceable records from the Helen Keller archives. Artists perished alongside their artifacts. Sculptor Michael Richards died as he worked in his studio on the 92nd floor of Tower One. His last work, now lost, was a statue commemorating the Tuskegee Airmen of World War II.

Of course, the loss of artifacts and art, no matter how priceless and precious, is dwarfed by the loss of life. Yet preserving and protecting our cultural holdings is of immense importance to civic life. Our cultural artifacts carry important messages about who we are and what we are defending. These irreplaceable objects are among our enemies' targets.

The Statue of Liberty, the Brooklyn and Bay Bridges, our skyscrapers, the Liberty Bell, our libraries and our schools are all potential targets--precisely because they stand as symbols of America's defining principles.

In light of that fact, today it is all the more urgent that we study American institutions, culture and history. Defending our democracy demands more than successful military campaigns. It also requires an understanding of the ideals, ideas and institutions that have shaped our country.

This is not a new concept. America's founders recognized the importance of an informed and educated citizenry as necessary for the survival of our participatory democracy. James Madison famously said, "The diffusion of knowledge is the only true guardian of liberty." Such knowledge tells us who we are as a people and why our country is worth fighting for. Such knowledge is part of our homeland defense.

Our values, ideas and collective memories are not self-sustaining. Just as free peoples must take responsibility for their own defense, they also must pass on to future generations the knowledge that sustains democracy.

It has been said that the erosion of freedom comes from three sources: from without, from within and from the passing of time. Though not as visible as marching armies, the injuries of time lead to the same outcome: a surrender of American ideals. Abraham Lincoln warned of this "silent artillery"--the fading memory of what we believe as Americans and why. And this loss of American memory has profound implications on our national security.

All great principles and institutions face challenges, and the wisdom of the humanities, and the pillars of democratic self-government, are not immune. We face a serious challenge to our country that lies within our borders--and even within our schools: the threat of American amnesia.

One of the common threads of great civilizations is the cultivation of memory. Many of the great works of antiquity are transliterated from oral traditions. From Homer to "Beowulf," such tales trained people to remember their heritage and history through story and song, and pass those stories and songs throughout generations. Old Testament stories repeatedly depict prophets and priests encouraging people to remember, to "write on their hearts" the events, circumstances and stories that make up their history.

We are in danger of forgetting this lesson. For years, even decades--polls, tests, and studies have shown that Americans do not know their history and cannot remember even the most significant events of the 20th century.

Of course, Americans are a forward-looking people. We are more concerned with what happens tomorrow than what happened yesterday. But we are in peril of having our view of the future obscured by our ignorance of the past. We cannot see clearly ahead if we are blind to history. Unfortunately, most indicators point to a worsening of our case of American amnesia.

I'll give just a few examples. One study of university students found that 40% could not place the Civil War in the correct half-century. Only 37% knew that the Battle of the Bulge took place during World War II. A national test of high school seniors found that 57% performed "below basic" level in American history. What does that mean? Well, over half of those tested couldn't say whom we fought in World War II. Eighteen percent believed that the Germans were our allies!

Such collective amnesia is dangerous. Citizens kept ignorant of their history are robbed of the riches of their heritage, and handicapped in their ability to understand and appreciate other cultures.

If Americans cannot recall whom we fought, and whom we fought alongside, during World War II, it should not be assumed that they will long remember what happened on September 11 or why we must be prepared and vigilant today. And a nation that does not know why it exists, or what it stands for, cannot be expected to long endure. As columnist George Will wrote, "We cannot defend what we cannot define."

Our nation's future depends on how we meet these challenges. We all have a stake, and a role to play, in recovering America's memory. There are several things we can do to alleviate our serious case of American amnesia.

This is where the National Endowment for the Humanities is answering the President's call to service. Announced by President Bush last September, the We the People initiative marks a systematic effort at the NEH to promote the study and understanding of American history and culture.

The President has requested $100 million over the next three years to support the initiative. If you watched and enjoyed Ken Burns's "The Civil War," you have seen the kind of public program we are supporting. We are working on equally (powerful) projects for museums, scholars, teachers and students. Young people will compete for $10,000 in prizes in the annual "Idea of America" essay contest. Other nationwide programs will reach students from kindergarten through college.

In the coming months and years, I want the NEH to help lead a renaissance in knowledge about our history and culture. We are the inheritors and guardians of a noble tradition, citizens of a democracy taking personal responsibility for our common defense. It is a heritage that extends back to the first democracies of Ancient Greece and runs through the whole history of our country.

Our values and traditions must be preserved and passed on. Without an active and informed citizenry, neither the toughest laws nor the strongest military can preserve our freedom. Knowing our nation's past, our founding ideas and our legacy of liberty is crucial to our homeland defense.

Our nation has faced many difficult challenges in the past, but, just as history teaches us to remain vigilant, it also shows us--with such vigilance--liberty and justice will prevail.

IMMIGRATION

The New Colossus
by Emma Lazarus

Not like the brazen giant of Greek fame
With conquering limbs astride from land to land;
Here at our sea-washed, sunset gates shall stand
A mighty woman with a torch, whose flame
Is the imprisoned lightning, and her name
Mother of Exiles. From her beacon-hand
Glows world-wide welcome; her mild eyes command
The air-bridged harbor that twin cities frame,
"Keep, ancient lands, your storied pomp!" cries she
With silent lips. "Give me your tired, your poor,
Your huddled masses yearning to breathe free,
The wretched refuse of your teeming shore,
Send these, the homeless, tempest-tossed to me,
I lift my lamp beside the golden door

The last few lines of Emma Lazarus' poem are well known as the inscription upon the Statute of Liberty, but the entire sonnet paints a fitting portrait of America's long history of embracing immigrants. The prospect of people leaving their homeland and journeying to an unfamiliar place to start anew is not exclusive to America's newcomers; throughout world history various factors have caused many to abandon their native lands. Still, there are major distinctions differentiating America from other countries in terms of the new arrivals. The massive amounts of sojourners who choose the United States as their new home and the successful way that these "foreigners" blend into the adopted nation stand out from the typical case of emigres.

Ethnic, civil, religous, and tribal strife are commonplace across the globe. Ongoing factionalism in Sudan claims thousands of lives every year. Recent history records genocidal battles in Rwanda, Serbia, Bosnia, Lebanon, The Ivory Coast, Russia, Chechnya, and on and on the list goes. Modern day Europe has seen a large increase of Middle Eastern immigrants recently, and sadly the continent has not adjusted peacefully. Combined with a resurgence in Europe's historic scourge of anti-Semitism, an uneasy miasma seems to be enveloping much of Europe and a future conflagration looks inevitable.

Amazingly despite the ubiquity of such apprehension toward foreigners, it has not plagued the United States--the one nation that welcomes more newcomers than virtually all the rest combined. Alarmists have always predicted hard times ahead for America's cohesion. Waves of Irish, Italian, and Jewish immigrants were originally viewed disdainfully in many circles. Japanese and Chinese newcomers were not fully welcomed when they started arriving in large numbers. Tocsins sounded that all these groups were deluging us and that they spoke a different language. Those same arguments are now often hurled against arrivals from Mexico and other Latin American countries. Valid concerns about people coming here illegally lose credibility when lumped in with xenophobic squawks about legal Latin American immigrants.

If history is any indication, these newcomers arriving now from every corner of the earth will fit in and benefit America while enjoying the many liberties available here. It may take a generation or two to master English--as it did for many of the previous arrivals, but immigrants founded America, and immigration has been one of the country's strengths since its inception.

Many of the quotes found on the following pages reveal the gratitude so many immigrants have for their new homeland, and others show how wise native-born Americans have always known that immigration is a very good thing--both for those blessed enough to get here and for America herself.

July 4, 1986 is a date I'll never forget. It was then that the Statue of Liberty ceremonies were held at Ellis Island and I was sworn in as a citizen.--Yakov Smirnoff, Immigrant from Russia when it was still part of the Soviet Union[1]

In gratitude to this adopted country of ours, I urge my Filipino brothers and sisters in America to support our soldiers. They are what the United States of America is made of, so that the immigrants, (like you and I) can fully live a life of freedom, and the people of the whole world can live as human beings.--Ofelia Bayutas Mutia, immigrant from the Phillipines[2]

Here (in America) individuals of all nations are melted into a new race of men, whose labors and posterity will one day cause great changes in the world.--Hector St. Jean de Crevecoeur in 1782

If they look back through this history to trace their connection with those days by blood, they find they have none; they cannot carry themselves back into that glorious epoch and make themselves feel that they are part of us. But when they look through that old Declaration of Independence, they find that those old men say that "We hold these truths to be self-evident, that all men are created equal," and then they feel that moral sentiment taught in that day evidences their relation to those men, that it is the father of all moral principle in them, and that they have a right to claim it as if they were blood of the blood, and flesh of the flesh, of the men who wrote that Declaration, and so they are.--Abraham Lincoln

The more I see of this country the more I feel I have to say thank you. This is the country of freedom and human rights.--Madalenna Lai, immigrant from Vietnam

I'm deeply grateful my immigrant grandparents were able to come to this country with nothing and make a good life. I benefited from that and was able to build upon the foundation they provided me to have a life of health and safety and opportunity.--Barbara Simpson [3]

Immigrants are exactly what America needs. They're what we need economically, and I think they're what we need morally ... [they] revitalize America and get it back to its sense of confidence... All of these immigrants that come here help us with the work they do, they challenge us with new ideas and new perspectives, and they give us perspective.--Rudolph Giuliani

The genius of the American experience has been the great leveling power. Human beings from a variety of cultures arrived here, collided, went to schools or wars together, married each other and built an amazing country.--Pete Hamill

Often citizenship given is undervalued, while citizenship earned is held in esteem.--Debra Saunders[4]

Those who realize the American dream have an obligation to further it with others.--Alphonso Jackson

The ideologues who proclaim the equality of all cultures simply cannot account for why so many people around the world would seem perfectly willing to dump their ancient cultures and adopt new ways that they associate with America.--Dinesh D'Souza, immigrant from India[5]

We can learn a lot from other countries, including how lucky we are to be Americans.--Thomas Sowell[6]

I was born and raised in Syria, the country enslaved by Hafez El-Assad. I was one of the fortunate victims of this tyranny because my family was able to emigrate to America, a land of freedom.
--Oubai Mohammad Shahbandar[7]

America is the one place where it is taboo to be proud of your culture, which is ironic given America's record as the freest, most prosperous and most benevolent society in world history.--David Limbaugh[8]

Emma Lazarus didn't say "send me your Harvard or Standford or MIT grads." She didn't say "send only your future entrepreneurs," or "your stars," or "your nobility," or your "best athletes." Instead she said to "give me your tired, poor and huddled masses." Even "wretched refuse." Because she understood how empowering freedom and opportunity can be to people.--Ralph F. Boyd, Jr.

Any success that I have achieved I owe to the opportunities and freedoms that America has given me.--Chirinjeev Kathuria, immigrant from India

So appealing is the idea of America that people continue to risk their lives on makeshift rafts to come across dangerous seas just to live here. They don't go to Saudi Arabia or Madagascar or Denmark or Brazil. --Daniel Flynn[9]

Americans tend to re-invent the world every five years, while Europeans are still fighting wars started centuries ago.--Vladimir Bukovsky, immigrant to England from Hungry[10]

Much less is it advisable for a person to go thither, who has no other quality to recommend him but his birth. In Europe it has indeed its value; but it is a commodity that cannot be carried to a worse market than that of America, where people do not inquire concerning a stranger, What is he? but, What can he do? If he has any useful art, he is welcome; and if he exercises it, and behaves well, he will be respected by all that know him.--Benjamin Franklin

We may have all come on different ships, but we're in the same boat now.--Martin Luther King, Jr.

Education, my father the grateful immigrant would say, was the glorious prize for growing up in America.--Suzanne Fields[11]

It's a privilege, a profound honor really, to serve your country in a time of crisis.--Viet Dinh, immigrant from Vietnam

The U.S.A. set an example to the world on how different races and different religions can coexist with respect despite their differences. --Nonie Darwish Middle Eastern immigrant[12]

The great social adventure of America is no longer the conquest of the wilderness but the absorption of fifty different peoples. --Walter Lippman.

Citizens by birth or choice of a common country, that country has a right to concentrate your affections. The name of American, which belongs to you, in your national capacity, must always exalt the just pride of Patriotism, more than any appellation derived from local discriminations.--George Washington

In those dark Soviet decades, cramped in the dusty communal apartments, surrounded by distorted mirrors of socialist propaganda, we knew that America existed. The smuggled pair of American jeans or the Simon and Garfunkel record was, for us, a symbol of civilization and freedom. We would go to suburban forests to listen to the "Voice of America" on short wave radios. The Soviets jammed it in the cities and spent more money on suppressing American radio than they spent on all their own broadcasting. The mere existence of America gave us the courage to fight.--Tatiana Menaker, immigrant from Russia when it was still part of the Soviet Union[13]

I am an immigrant who became a US Citizen over 20 years ago and I share the values and desires of many of this nation's immigrants. Most people who come to this country want to work hard and succeed in the American system; the Congress needs to implement policies that encourage productivity and success. President Bush's recent guest-worker proposal is a fair policy, but is contingent upon enforcement of immigration law, which has been ineffective up to this point. Legal immigration is undermined by illegal immigration. Moreover, illegal immigrants are disadvantaged by their illegal status, and it is not right that our government has allowed them to come and live here under such circumstances.--Claudia Bermudez, immigrant from Nicaragua

By the time I got my citizenship in 1964, I was grateful and immensely proud to be told by the judge in grand rapids, Michigan that I would not be a Hungarian-American, nor any other hyphenated American. While no one suggested then, or has since, that I disown or forget my upbringing, I was now simply and officially, American.
--Balint Vazsonyi[14]

We were dark-skinned Cubans, who still did not command the language or the culture of our new country. Who knows what the KKK would do to us after we had left the haven of Miami to move to the "sticks" of South Carolina? After all, this was 1968 and race riots were in full swing. But the Southern people we were supposed to fear welcomed us with open arms. We were treated very well in Columbia, South Carolina.--Miguel Faria[15]

We are a nation, not a hodge-podge of foreign nationalities. We are a people, and not a polyglot boarding house.--Theodore Roosevelt

We are assimilating ourselves. Now there are plenty of middle-class Latinos to model ourselves after, not unlike other immigrant groups.
--Gregory Rodriguez.

Here is not merely a nation but a teeming nation of nations.
--Walt Whitman

We may like to think we are all rugged American individuals, making our own choices immune to the opinions of others. But all you have to do is talk to somebody from another country and hear him say "all you Americans are alike" to understand how powerful the common culture really is.--Jonah Goldberg[16]

Throughout my life, I have witnessed the greatness of America, and the genuine goodness of the American people.--Mel Martinez, immigrant from Cuba

For a hundred years, Lady Liberty adorned this harbor and has beckoned new Americans. Her promise is that when people are allowed to breathe the air of freedom, to exercise themselves and their talents in an environment of opportunities, that there is no limit to the heights to which individuals can rise.--John Ashcroft

Through multiculturalism, cultural relativism and a therapeutic curriculum our schools often promote the very values from which new immigrants are fleeing -- tribalism, statism and group rather than individual interests....There is a reason, after all, why those in a rather cold and inhospitable Canada, north of the Dakotas and Minnesota, do not cross into America by the millions, while others from a temperate, naturally beautiful, oil-rich, mineral-laden, and fertile Mexico do. --Victor Davis Hanson[17]

Immigrants who come here from around the world with every desire and intention to become Americans may be hijacked by those activists who are ideologically committed to keeping them speaking foreign languages, loyal to foreign value and -- if possible -- taught to feel historic grievances against the country that is welcoming them today. --Thomas Sowell[18]

I have always believed that there was some divine plan that placed this great continent between two oceans to be sought out by those who were possessed of an abiding love of freedom and a special kind of courage. This was true of those who pioneered the great wilderness in the beginning of this country, as it is also true of those later immigrants who were willing to leave the land of their birth and come to a land where even the language was unknown to them.--Ronald Reagan

I love America; I am the American Dream.--Marshall Kim, Immigrant from Cambodia

I've lived in this country much longer than I lived in Laos so right now I feel that everything here is home.--Chaxiong Lo, Hmong Immigrant

The American Dream to me is to become an American citizen to get that respect from Americans.--Jose Velasquez, immigrant from El Salvador

Henry Miller said that the problem with native people is that they don't look at the monuments in their own towns. I do. As an immigrant, I appreciate every inch I have gained.-- Shohreh Aghdashloo, immigrant from Iran[19]

My family was given a home in America. I joined the military to thank America. There are parts of the Middle East policy that I disagree with. But just because you're angry over policies, don't ask me to take off the uniform.--Gunnery Sergeant Jamal Baadani, immigrant from Egypt

Now that I am a citizen of this great country, it makes me proud to think of myself as one of America's people. Right after I was sworn in, I felt like I'd just been given a lifetime membership to the greatest country club in the world.--Yakov Smirnoff[20]

The section devoted to September 11, 2001 entailed how much good can often be derived from unfathomable evil. In this speech President George W. Bush addressed another instance where immeasurable horror ultimately led to redemption. To most newcomers the journey to America is the fulfillment of fervent hopes, but sadly there was a class of immigrants who stood as a glaring exception to that rule. On July 8, 2003 while on a visit to Goree Island off the coast of Senegal President Bush spoke of the depravity inflicted upon people who emigrated against their will via the iniquitous slave trade. His thoughtful words describe how America eventually purged itself of this sin and how the descendents of many of those poor souls have gleaned rich rewards while simultaneously enriching their homeland.

Remarks of President George W. Bush on Goree Island, Senegal, July 8, 2003

Mr. President and Madam First Lady (Senegal's Abdoulaye and Viviane Wade), distinguished guests and residents of Goree Island, citizens of Senegal, I'm honored to begin my visit to Africa in your beautiful country.

For hundreds of years on this island peoples of different continents met in fear and cruelty. Today we gather in respect and friendship, mindful of past wrongs and dedicated to the advance of human liberty.

At this place, liberty and life were stolen and sold. Human beings were delivered and sorted, and weighed, and branded with the marks of commercial enterprises, and loaded as cargo on a voyage without return. One of the largest migrations of history was also one of the greatest crimes of history.

Below the decks, the middle passage was a hot, narrow, sunless nightmare; weeks and months of confinement and abuse and confusion on a strange and lonely sea. Some refused to eat, preferring death to any future their captors might prepare for them. Some who were sick were thrown over the side. Some rose up in violent rebellion, delivering the closest thing to justice on a slave ship. Many acts of defiance and bravery are recorded. Countless others, we will never know.

Those who lived to see land again were displayed, examined, and sold at auctions across nations in the Western Hemisphere. They entered societies indifferent to their anguish and made prosperous by their unpaid labor. There was a time in my country's history when one in every seven human beings was the property of another. In law, they were regarded only as articles of commerce, having no right to travel, or to marry, or to own possessions. Because families were often separated, many (were)denied even the comfort of suffering together.

For 250 years the captives endured an assault on their culture and their dignity. The spirit of Africans in America did not break. Yet the spirit of their captors was corrupted. Small men took on the powers and airs of tyrants and masters. Years of unpunished brutality and bullying and rape produced a dullness and hardness of conscience. Christian men and women became blind to the clearest commands of their faith and added hypocrisy to injustice. A republic founded on equality for all became a prison for millions. And yet in the words of the African proverb, "no fist is big enough to hide the sky." All the generations of oppression under the laws of man could not crush the hope of freedom and defeat the purposes of God.

In America, enslaved Africans learned the story of the exodus from Egypt and set their own hearts on a promised land of freedom. Enslaved Africans discovered a suffering Savior and found he was more like themselves than their masters. Enslaved Africans heard the ringing promises of the Declaration of Independence and asked the self-evident question, then why not me?

In the year of America's founding, a man named Olaudah Equiano was taken in bondage to the New World. He witnessed all of slavery's cruelties, the ruthless and the petty. He also saw beyond the slave-holding piety of the time to a higher standard of humanity. "God tells us," wrote Equiano, "that the oppressor and the oppressed are both in His hands. And if these are not the poor, the broken-hearted, the blind, the captive, the bruised which our Savior speaks of, who are they?"

Down through the years, African Americans have upheld the ideals of America by exposing laws and habits contradicting those ideals. The rights of African Americans were not the gift of those in authority. Those rights were granted by the Author of Life, and regained by the persistence and courage of African Americans, themselves.

Among those Americans was Phyllis Wheatley, who was dragged from her home here in West Africa in 1761, at the age of seven. In my country, she became a poet, and the first noted black author in our nation's history. Phyllis Wheatley said, "In every human breast, God has implanted a principle which we call love of freedom. It is impatient of oppression and pants for deliverance."

That deliverance was demanded by escaped slaves named Frederick Douglass and Sojourner Truth, educators named Booker T. Washington and W.E.B. DuBois, and ministers of the Gospel named Leon Sullivan and Martin Luther King, Jr. At every turn, the struggle for equality was resisted by many of the powerful. And some have said we should not judge their failures by the standards of a later time. Yet, in every time, there were men and women who clearly saw this sin and called it by name.

We can fairly judge the past by the standards of President John Adams, who called slavery "an evil of colossal magnitude." We can discern eternal standards in the deeds of William Wilberforce and John Quincy Adams, and Harriet Beecher Stowe, and Abraham Lincoln. These men and women, black and white, burned with a zeal for freedom, and they left behind a different and better nation. Their moral vision caused Americans to examine our hearts, to correct our Constitution, and to teach our children the dignity and equality of every person of every race. By a plan known only to Providence, the stolen sons and daughters of Africa helped to awaken the conscience of America. The very people traded into slavery helped to set America free.

My nation's journey toward justice has not been easy and it is not over. The racial bigotry fed by slavery did not end with slavery or with segregation. And many of the issues that still trouble America have roots in the bitter experience of other times. But however long the journey, our destination is set: liberty and justice for all.

In the struggle of the centuries, America learned that freedom is not the possession of one race. We know with equal certainty that freedom is not the possession of one nation. This belief in the natural rights of man, this conviction that justice should reach wherever the sun passes leads America into the world.

With the power and resources given to us, the United States seeks to bring peace where there is conflict, hope where there is suffering, and liberty where there is tyranny. And these commitments bring me and other distinguished leaders of my government across the Atlantic to Africa.

African peoples are now writing your own story of liberty. Africans have overcome the arrogance of colonial powers, overturned the cruelties of apartheid, and made it clear that dictatorship is not the future of any nation on this continent. In the process, Africa has produced heroes of liberation--leaders like Mandela, Senghor, Nkrumah, Kenyatta, Selassie and Sadat. And many visionary African leaders, such as my friend, have grasped the power of economic and political freedom to lift whole nations and put forth bold plans for Africa's development.

Because Africans and Americans share a belief in the values of liberty and dignity, we must share in the labor of advancing those values. In a time of growing commerce across the globe, we will ensure that the nations of Africa are full partners in the trade and prosperity of the world. Against the waste and violence of civil war, we will stand together for peace. Against the merciless terrorists who threaten every nation, we will wage an unrelenting campaign of justice. Confronted with desperate hunger, we will answer with human compassion and the tools of human technology. In the face of spreading disease, we will join with you in turning the tide against AIDS in Africa.

We know that these challenges can be overcome, because history moves in the direction of justice. The evils of slavery were accepted and unchanged for centuries. Yet, eventually, the human heart would not abide them. There is a voice of conscience and hope in every man and woman that will not be silenced--what Martin Luther King called a certain kind of fire that no water could put out. That flame could not be extinguished at the Birmingham jail. It could not be stamped out at Robben Island Prison. It was seen in the darkness here at Goree Island, where no chain could bind the soul. This untamed fire of justice continues to burn in the affairs of man, and it lights the way before us.

May God bless you all.

EGALITARIANISM

It is not tolerance that one is entitled to in America. It is the right of every citizen to be treated by other citizens as an equal.--Wendell Wilkie

That a persistent wave of immigration has made America the world's Great Melting Pot is amazing in its own right, but even more significant is the spirit of egalitarianism that permeates the land affording every American unlimited opportunities.

Without any planning, organization, or probably even not much awareness the United States became the prototype where people from every background effortlessly intermingle, and it succeeded unimaginably. As mentioned in the immigration introduction the routine harmony stands in stark contrast to virtually every other country where different ethnicities live. Beyond the lack of discord lies a chance for each American--regardless of race, class, or other characteristics to succeed by surmounting whatever obstacles arise.

Sadly for much of our history there were elements of society that didn't embrace the true American Egalitarian spirit. The legality of slavery for eighty-six years of our nation's existence will forever stand as a demerit in our history, but America obliterated the scourge from its borders--unlike much of the world. Today an estimated twenty-five million people remain trapped in slavery across the globe.

Artificial barriers no longer inhibit anyone from pursuing the American Dream, but new forces now try to erect nefarious hurdles. The unctuous twin fads of multiculturalism and diversity seek to label people by categories and foster the very Balkanization that we so impressively have avoided here. While they are arguably well-intentioned notions, the supremacy of racial or ethnic components as deciding factors was also the guiding principle of the Ku Klux Klan, and even such innocuously named sequestering strategies must be relegated to history's ash heap. The truly American way treats everyone as an individual and understands that skin color and national ancestry are irrelevant in influencing a person's worth.

Racial strife is not yet totally nonexistent, but institutional discrimination is a thing of the past. Fortunately most Americans realize what truly matters, and the vast majority of us evaluate each other based on the content of our character not the color of our skin. Many notable Americans aided us as we improved our commitment to equality. The egalitarianism exhibited by Abraham Lincoln, Susan B. Anthony, Martin Luther King, Jr., Michael Schwerner, Andy Goodman, and James Chaney and several other famous folk cannot be overestimated, but many ordinary Americans whose names will never be recorded in history books quietly treated all their fellow citizens as God's children and helped equality become a bedrock of Americanism.

Although no effort was made to be "inclusive" in compiling this chapter's quotes, a pretty "diverse" assortment of speakers is featured. Some of the quotes are from the Founding Fathers and show a tactile awareness that slavery-- although institutionalized worldwide at the time--was a grave evil. Others are early Americans who demonstrated a virtuous spirit of equality before it was the cultural norm.

In this country we have no place for hyphenated Americans.
--Theodore Roosevelt

Under the name of racial diversity, however, it appears that the value of true diversity of opinion is ignored, and free speech is attacked. Blacks, Asians, and Hispanics who espouse conservative views are called ugly names--whites who espouse conservative views are, regardless of facts, called racists.--David Wienir[1]

I got a simple rule about everybody. If you don't treat me right--shame on you!--Louis Armstrong

We have seen the mere distinction of color made, in the most enlightened period of time, a ground of the most oppressive dominion ever exercised by man over man.--James Madison

A new intolerance divides us by Race and Gender and Ethnicity and Language, and into Minority and Majority, and generally makes many out of one, reversing that most American of mottos, E Pluribus Unum.--Paul Greenburg[2]

It was not for their own land they fought, not even for a land which had adopted them, but for a land which had enslaved them and whose laws under even in freedom oftener oppressed than protected. Bravery under such circumstances has a peculiar beauty and merit.--Harriet Beecher Stowe on Black Revolutionary War soldiers

Through a mistaken policy you have heretofore been deprived of participation in the glorious struggle for national rights in which our country is engaged. This no longer shall exist.--Andrew Jackson addressing black soldiers during the War of 1812

All the army made history during the short Cuban war but the colored regulars in three days practically revolutionized the sentiment of the country in regard to the colored soldier.--Theophilus G. Steward during the Spanish American War

They are not surpassed by any seamen we have in this fleet and I have yet to learn that the color of a man's skin or the cut and trimmings of the coat can affect a man's qualifications or usefulness.--Commodore Isaac Chauncey commenting on black soldiers during the War of 1812

Yesterday, I secured a decision from the High Command which I think is the greatest since the enactment of the Constitutional Amendments following the Emancipation.--General Benjamin O. Davis, Sr. on the ruling allowing black troops to volunteer for combat duty

In recognizing the humanity of our fellow beings, we pay ourselves the highest tribute.--Thurgood Marshall

Cultural diversity or multiculturalism in the schools is hip and trendy, but most attitudes are rooted in the home. We won't change them by merely celebrating different food days or holidays.--Suzanne Fields[3]

Each and every one of you is a child of God, put on this Earth not to destroy one another, but put on this Earth to love one another, believe in one another, and work for the cause of peace.--Colin Powell

I don't think of myself as Arab-American but as an American of Arab ancestry.--Sergeant Omar Masry

We cannot stop professional racists from stirring even imaginary pots as they try to keep their jobs, but we should remember that the road to better race relations lies where it always has: Looking at each other as human beings and not as representatives of groups or classes. --Charley Reese

The notion that race determines thinking was a notion that should have been buried in a Berlin bunker 50 years ago.--William Bennett

Every day our nation was segregated was a day that America was unfaithful to our founding ideals.--George W. Bush

As Americans we have to confront issues of race and class honestly and forthrightly. But we've just got to stop reflexively resorting to victim politics. We can't continue to condition--through our discourse about race--condition our African American young people so that when they look in the mirror they see a victim.--Ralph F. Boyd, Jr.

Our Constitution is color-blind, and neither knows nor tolerates classes among citizens.--John Harlan

I can only say that there is not a man living who wishes more sincerely than I do to see a plan adopted for the abolition of it [slavery]; but there is only one proper and effectual mode by which it can be accomplished, and that is by Legislative authority; and this, as far as my suffrage will go, shall never be wanting.--George Washington

There is not a Black America and a White America and Latino America and Asian America; there's the United States of America. --Barack Obama

Blacks were not in Vietnam because an evil government drafted them out of the ghettoes to use as cannon fodder; they were there because of the courage and patriotism of young black men despite the fact that they frequently experienced racism.--B. G. Burkett[5]

The Africans, and the blacks in servitude among us, were really as much included in these assertions (enunciated in the Declaration of Independence) as ourselves; and their right, unalienable right to liberty, and to procure and possess property, is as much asserted as ours. --Stephen Hopkins

That men should pray and fight for their own freedom and yet keep others in slavery is certainly acting a very inconsistent as well as unjust and perhaps impious part.--John Jay

We must all use restraint in our use of the various "isms." --Heather McCormick[6]

The government of the United States is a device for maintaining in perpetuity the rights of the people, with the ultimate extinction of all privileged classes.--Calvin Coolidge

The Federal Government was never in its essence anything but anti-slavery...If in its origin, slavery had any relation to the government, it was only as the scaffolding to the magnificent structure, to be removed as soon as the building was completed.--Frederick Douglass

You must remember that the President is their President too.
--Eleanor Roosevelt

Unlike other nations, American identity is not based on ethnicity or geography. It's based on a moral proposition. This proposition comes straight from the faded and yellowed document: The Declaration of Independence.--Chuck Colson

An ethnically 'diverse' student enrollment, no matter how it is eventually achieved, may not even begin to reflect the diversity that actually exists within groups.--Isabelle Quinn[7]

Holding fellow men in bondage and slavery is repugnant to the golden law of God and the inalienable right of mankind as well as every principle of the late glorious revolution.--Philip Graham upon freeing his slaves in 1787

Slavery is repugnant to the principles of Christianity. It is rebellion again the authority of a common Father. It is a practical denial of the extent and efficacy of the death of a common Savior. It is an usurpation of the prerogative of the great Sovereign of the universe who has solemnly claimed an exclusive property in the souls of men.--Benjamin Rush

Why keep alive the question of slavery? It is admitted by all to be a great evil.--Charles Carroll

I will permit no man to narrow and degrade my soul by making me hate him.----Booker T. Washington

Enlisted men--blacks and whites--live in the same barracks, eat in the same mess halls, and although not required, frequently at the same table--something rarely encountered in universities.--Walter Berns[8]

(Sweedish born Economist) Gunnar Myrdal had suggested in 1944 that traditional American values were the greatest foes of racism because they emphasized equality and liberty--values inherently in contradiction to policies of segregation and exclusion.
--Charles J. Sykes[9]

How well I recall the smell of the rich earth. I can see my little brother and me playing with a black boy and his sister, the children of tenant farmers on the place my dad had rented...We had such a good time but when company came to their house or to our house we had to break up the fun and go our separate ways...Oh I used to be furious about this and I would argue with my dad no end. "When you're older you will understand," he told me. I'm eighty-one, and I still don't understand.
 --Dale Evans10

Ideas themselves have neither color nor ethnicity.--Gregory Kane

"Charlie" was the enemy, and olive green was the only color that mattered.--David Parks on the attitude of soldiers during the Vietnam War[11]

Distinctions by race are so evil, so arbitrary, and invidious that a state, bound to defend the equal protection of the laws must not invoke them in any public sphere.--Thurgood Marshall

Anti-American sentiment, refusal to assimilate, and separatist ethnic identity politics do untold damage to our schools and to our country, generally harming minorities most of all.--Marc Bereley[12]

I do not despair of this country. There are forces in operation, which must inevitably work for the downfall of slavery.--Frederick Douglass

Every day I wake up and find more things about America that I love. --Sarah Saga

There should be neither slavery nor involuntary servitude in any of the states.--Rufus King

Our history must acknowledge that America has always had a contingent of whites fighting for black dignity.--John McWhorter[13]

The work of cultural unity is of the ages; advancing racial and ethnic separatism is a gesture of the moment.--Victor Davis Hanson[14]

The strength of our Nation must continue to be used in the interest of all our people rather than a privileged few. It must continue to be used unselfishly in the struggle for world peace and the betterment of mankind.--Harry Truman

I wish most sincerely that there was not a slave in the province. It always seemed a most iniquitous scheme to me--to fight ourselves for what we are daily robbing and plundering from those who have as good a right to freedom as we have. You know my mind on this subject.--Abigail Adams

How exactly is a nation that cherishes "inalienable rights" and codifies its most sacred beliefs about government and its people in a "Bill of Rights" in any way equal to cultures that are built on brutality and intolerance?--Bernard Goldberg[15]

One of the most disturbing facets of the whole multicultural fad is the arbitrary labels it inflicts upon all Americans. The first quote in this section by Theodore Roosevelt disparages the divisive notion of "hyphenated Americans." The idea of putting some modifier in front of "American," while currently in vogue in some circles, suggests a lesser form of citizen than a non-hyphenated American.

Ironically, universities, corporations, and government bureaucracies are placing more and more emphasis on these amorphous categorizations, but ordinary Americans have overwhelmingly adopted a colorblind attitude. Most of us regret the period in our country's proud history when skin color was weighed as a pertinent factor and realize that the genuine American experience celebrates individual contributions. While such egalitarian attitudes are refreshingly common now, few could promulgate the point as eloquently as Eric L. Strickland's accompanying treatise does. The brilliant narrative, which invokes the memory of Martin Luther King, Jr. and Abraham Lincoln, displays a rhetorical adroitness that matches the finest presentations of these two renowned orators. More importantly it is safe to say that these great Americans-both of whom gave their lives in the fight for equality--would enthusiastically endorse its empowering thesis. Many of us may be similarly living out Mr. Strickland's (and Reverend King's) dream, but rarely has it been articulated with such coruscating suasion. This essay first appeared in the Pittsburgh Post-Gazette on August 23, 2003--the 40th anniversary of Martin Luther King, Jr.'s "I Have a Dream" Speech.

Forty Years after Martin Luther King, Jr.'s Landmark Speech, I Have a Dream, Too
by Eric L. Striickland

Two score years ago, a great American, in whose symbolic shadow we now live, stood upon the steps of the Lincoln Memorial and issued a decree to all Americans. In his speech, he mentioned "Negroes" and "Americans" and his desire that one day the two should become one. In 1963, Martin Luther King, Jr. felt it was time "to lift our nation from the quicksand of racial injustice to the solid rock of brotherhood." One brotherhood.

It seems to me that no matter where I go or what I do, I am a hyphenated American. If I were to become the first of anything, I would invariably be called the first African-American to achieve this stature. When one black achieves a goal, that person must then wear the crown of de facto representative for the entire race. This is seen not only in the nomenclature of first African-American, but also in the fact that he or she will immediately be asked questions such as "How does this help the African-American community?" or "As an African-American, how do you feel?" And, sometimes grievously for us all, this person will be catapulted into the position of role model and canon bearer.

The role of First African-American carries with it a tremendous burden. That burden is placed there by media, by our peers and by blacks in general. We are immediately painted with the brush of ethnicity instead of being written with the ink of individuality. Our accomplishments, once our own, soon become the proprietorship of the entire black community. The achievement of the black individual becomes the communal glory of the black race. This becomes a burden only in that the individual is now viewed as part of the whole. He or she loses distinctiveness and is soon enshrouded with the appellation African-American.

The very way we achieved our goal becomes a possible burden. On the one hand, one can never be seen as having used race to achieve a position. If that happens, the more outspoken and vociferous blacks will refer to them as "house niggers" who are only there at the behest of their masters. However, if one were to achieve a position through sheer dogged determination, then they can never "deny their race." They must not only be proud of their race; they must trumpet that fact wherever they go. To do otherwise would be to sell out the race that supposedly got them where they are today.

I dream of a world in which I go to the polls and vote American. I dream of a world in which there is no official or unofficial spokesman for African-Americans. I dream of a world in which all blacks have removed the hyphenation that is roped around our necks like an albatross.

However, there are those who would say that it's necessary to continue to delineate ourselves. They would say that we must unite and speak with one voice. They would say that we must accept our heritage and that attempting to remove ourselves from the community would be wrong. They would say that anything other than attempting to live up to the expectations of our forefathers and current leaders would be wrong.

And, I would agree with them. However, I would say that those things must be done as Americans! As Americans, we must unite and speak with one voice! Because we are American, we must strive to live up to the values that our country is built upon. Martin Luther King in his speech said, "We cannot walk alone." And, in that same oration, he stated that his dream was "a dream deeply rooted in the American dream."

Yes, I agree that there are times in which various segments--even races--of society must unite in order to achieve a goal. However, when I am led to believe that all my thoughts, hopes and beliefs must be based on one aspect of my life--my color--then I will forever rebel. Having to accept blindly the choices of others is as repulsive to me as slavery! When I am told that I should vote a certain way, or accept a certain position, or promote a certain idea just because I am black, am I not being mentally shackled with a form of ethnic slavery? And, it matters not if it be the NAACP, the Urban League or any other organization that supports this idea, I cannot and will not be bound by ethnicity. Binding does not free.

I want to be known only as an American. And, if one day I achieve great status in America, I want to be known only as an American. And, if one day I become a malefactor and scourge to society who is unworthy of any compassion, I want to be known only as an American. And, if one day you see me and I'm listening to rap or country, if I've just voted Republican or Democrat, if I'm rich or poor, if I'm smart or lacking in intelligence, see me only as an American.

When that happens, I will know that I live in a free society based not upon the color of my skin, but upon the content of my character.

THE RIGHT TO VOTE

The ballot box is the surest arbiter of disputes among freemen.--James Buchanan

In a surreal moment during a 2003 television interview, Saddam Hussein told Dan Rather that in his recent "reelection" he had garnered 100% of the vote. This fabricated electoral "triumph" appeared to truly impress the naive newscaster, but for many observers it was cause for us to stop and realize how lucky we are to live in the United States.

The preposterousness of the dictator's boast highlights one of America's most alluring attributes--one completely unknown to much of the world--the right to vote in free and fair elections. Even if Hussein had achieved a perfect reelection tally, he had no opponents because he prevented others from challenging him. The Iraqi people had a choice--not between candidates; they could choose to vote for their reigning despot (the only name on the ballot) or face arrest, torture, and likely execution by abstaining from casting a ballot. Iraq under Saddam was hardly unique in its denial of a right Americans take for granted (and too many apathetically avoid.)

Cuba, Zimbabwe, North Korea, Sudan, and Vietnam are just a few of the innumerable places where authentic elections are nonexistent. Even when sham voting procedures are staged, the process is typified by rampant fraud. Russia, where democratization looked so promising just a decade ago, recently held an election where one of the most promising challengers mysteriously disappeared a few weeks prior to balloting, and the authorities took few steps to investigate the curious development. In 2004 the Ukrainian people only saw a genuine election after massive nationwide protests made crystal clear that the farcical balloting the government initially staged would not stand. In the Palestinian territories the late terrorist honcho Yassir Arafat's sole opponent was once an octogenarian woman with no political experience who had endorsed Arafat.

In America the right to vote existed sparingly at first. While sporadic locales let black men vote from the time the Constitution was ratified, originally the right was officially denied to all but white men. Yet like so many other wrongs in America's past, the nation corrected itself. Today millions of naturalized immigrants vote for candidates of their choice--a simple but empowering activity that many never could have dreamt of undertaking back in their native lands.

The basic right and sacred privilege to vote has been completely unknown to much of humanity throughout mankind's history. Many, many people have lived their entire lives without ever a casting an authentic ballot.

In the year 2000, America experienced it closest presidential election ever due primarily to the nearly identical numbers of votes cast for each candidate in Florida. Even after the Supreme Court ruled for the apparent victor, some still disputed the result until numerous unofficial tallies were conducted of Florida's votes that conclusively proved that the valid winner was in office. For the duration of the controversy, a heated debate energetically ensued, but not a single shot was fired. No lives were lost in the contentious legal battle whose outcome would have far reaching goals, and the specter of martial law was never even considered. The peaceful transfer of power under the best circumstances is rare around the world, but unrest did not befall America even during what would have proven to be a national crisis just about anywhere else.

On Election Day this year as you walk into the voting booth, stop for just one moment to contemplate what you are doing. Your voice will be heard among the multitudes as you carry on another one of the great traditions that makes America the Sweet Land of Liberty.

Hopefully the words of the quoted individuals in this section will help us all appreciate how special our right to vote truly is and counteract the parlous indifference that too many Americans demonstrate toward voting.

The vote is the most powerful instrument ever devised by man for breaking down injustice and destroying the terrible walls which imprison men because they are different from other men. --Lyndon Johnson

I shall here, perhaps, be reminded of a current observation, "that where annual elections end, tyranny begins."--James Madison

America's the greatest country in the world and will remain so if Americans take seriously their right and responsibility to vote. If you care about our culture, and the values we pass on to our children, about our country, then vote Tuesday and ask your friends and family to vote too.--George W. Bush

No one party can fool all of the people all of the time; that's why we have two parties.--Bob Hope

The ignorance of one voter in a democracy impairs the security of all.--John F. Kennedy

The vote demonstrates that we accept the notion that all human beings are created in the image of God and have an equal right to preach and teach the word of God.--Alexander M. Shapiro

In an American election, there are no losers, because whether or not our candidates are successful, the next morning we all wake up as Americans. That is the greatest privilege and the most remarkable good fortune that can come to us on Earth. --John Kerry

No man will ever bring out of the Presidency the reputation which carries him into it.--Thomas Jefferson

Society in every state is a blessing, but government, even in its best state, is but a necessary evil; in its worst state an intolerable one.--Thomas Paine

The ballot is stronger than the bullet.--Abraham Lincoln

The right to vote is not just any ordinary right—it is the essential, defining ingredient of a democracy.-- Alan W. Dowd[1]

Elections are a human endeavor and, as such, can never be totally error-free. Yet every eligible voter had the opportunity to vote, using regular or provisional ballots. Was the process perfect? No. But it was perfectly inspiring—a testament to the strength and power of our democratic system, the commitment of American voters to have their voices heard and the integrity of the process that encouraged participation and demanded fairness.--Kenneth Blackwell on Ohio's much-scrutinized 2004 presidential election

Vote: The only commodity that is peddleable without a license. --Mark Twain

Always vote for principle, though you may vote alone, and you may cherish the sweetest reflection that your vote is never lost. --John Quincy Adams

The idea that you can merchandise candidates for high office like breakfast cereal--that you can gather votes like box tops-- is, I think, the ultimate indignity to the democratic process. --Adlai Stevenson

I urge all the voters of our country, without reference to party, that they assemble tomorrow at their respective voting places in the exercise of the high office of American citizenship, that they approach the ballot box in the spirit that they would approach a sacrament.--Calvin Coolidge

Count first and rule upon legality afterwards is not a recipe for producing election results that have the public acceptance democratic stability requires.--Antonin Scalia

When you become entitled to exercise the right of voting for public officers, let it be impressed on your mind that God commands you to choose for rulers just men who will rule in the fear of God. The preservation of a republican government depends on the faithful discharge of this duty.--Noah Webster

The Electoral College respects the regional complexity and diversity of the United States. By giving weight (as the US Senate also does) to less populated areas, it acts as a block against conspiratorial machinations and peer pressure in overpopulated metropolises.--Camille Paglia[2]

The future of this republic is in the hands of the American voter. --Dwight D. Eisenhower

When a fellow tells me he's bipartisan, I know he's going to vote against me.--Harry Truman

Perhaps America will one day go fascist democratically, by popular vote.--William Shirer

Do not run a campaign that would embarrass your mother. --Robert Byrd

If God had wanted us to vote, he would have given us candidates. --Jay Leno

If elected I shall be thankful; if not, it will be all the same. --Abraham Lincoln

Finishing second in the Olympics gets you silver. Finishing second in politics gets you oblivion.--Richard Nixon

An election cannot give a country a firm sense of direction if it has two or more national parties which merely have different names, but are as alike in their principles and aims as two peas in the same pod.--Franklin Delano Roosevelt

There is no excitement anywhere in the world, short of war, to match the excitement of the American presidential campaign. --Theodore White

A citizen of America will cross the ocean to fight for democracy, but won't cross the street to vote in a national election. --Bill Vaughn

Bad officials are elected by good citizens who do not vote. --George Jean Nathan

Giving every man a vote has no more made men wise and free than Christianity has made them good.--H. L. Mencken

Suffrage is the pivotal right.--Susan B. Anthony

The fact that a man is to vote forces him to think. You may preach to a congregation by the year and not affect its thought because it is not called upon for definite action. But throw your subject into a campaign and it becomes a challenge.--John Jay Chapman

Your every voter, as surely as your chief magistrate, exercises a public trust.--Grover Cleveland

A straw vote only shows which way the hot air blows.--O. Henry

If our vote doesn't count for anything, we've lost our Republic. --Jack Adsit

All voting is a sort of gaming, like checkers or backgammon, with a slight moral tinge to it, a playing with right and wrong. --Henry David Thoreau

The rhetoric that leaders use to describe their nations tells you a great deal about those nations. And no other nation's leaders use this goodness terminology nearly as often as American leaders (of both political parties) do.--Dennis Prager[3]

My opponent called me a cream puff. Well, I rushed out and got the baker's union to endorse me.--Claiborne Pell

Voters don't decide issues, they decide who will decide issues.--George Will

Republics are created by the virtue, public spirit, and intelligence of the citizens. They fall, when the wise are banished from the public councils, because they dare to be honest, and the profligate are rewarded, because they flatter the people, in order to betray them.--Joseph Story

Now more that ever before, the people are responsible for the character of their Congress. If that body be ignorant, reckless, and corrupt, it is because the people tolerate ignorance, recklessness, and corruption. If the next centennial does not find us a great nation...it will be because those who represent the enterprise, the culture, and the morality of the nation do not aid in controlling the political forces.--James Garfield

Presidential elections are already just about as democratic as they can be. We already have one man, one vote--but in the states. Elections are as freely and democratically contested as elections can be--but in the states. Victory always goes democratically to the winner of the raw popular vote--but in the states.--Martin Diamond

No higher or more assuring proof could exist of the strength and permanence of popular government than the fact that though the chosen of the people be struck down, his constitutional successor is peacefully installed without shock or strain.--Chester A. Arthur

Prior to the nail biter we witnessed on Election Night 2000 a significant portion of Americans were probably not well-versed with the Electoral College. Some who had a scant familiarity with the term wondered just what degree programs were offered there and where its campus was located. Sadly even now with stories about this non-accredited "college" faded from the daily headlines, too many Americans fail to understand the ingenuity our Founders demonstrated when they concocted such an abstruse method of tabulating national vote totals. Calls to abolish the complicated "college" have recurred incessantly since shortly after its inception, but wise Americans realize its intrinsic value, and maintaining the fairest possible system of national elections has always triumphed over fleeting political calculations and the desire for simplicity. In this brief essay, syndicated columnist Mike North perspicuously explains just how the Electoral College operates and why it is an asset to our country. Beyond the practical purposes it serves this bizarre vote-counting arrangement is a truly American initiative and stands as an important example of the seminal wizardry that has long existed within our borders. The essay was first published on September 3, 2004.

In Defense Of The Electoral College
by Mike North

As the election nears, we are again hearing notes of discord regarding our method of electing a President. The Electoral College must go, we're told.

A study by the American Council of Trustees and Alumni indicated that 81% of college seniors made a "D" or an "F" on a high school level history exam. How can these students understand or appreciate the sheer genius behind our system of government if they don't know the reasoning behind it?

Our view of the present depends on our knowledge of history. We hear references on CNN to the Electoral College as a system whose time may have passed. If we know no better, we accept what we hear from these talking heads. But the Electoral College is our Founders' guarantee of protection against the mob rule of unrestrained democracy.

Though many people wish it were so, America is not a pure democracy. James Madison, principal author of the Constitution, wrote, "democracies have ever been spectacles of turbulence and contention; have ever been found incompatible with personal security or the rights of property; and have in general been as short in their lives as they have been violent in their deaths."

Democracy has been described as two wolves and one sheep voting on what to have for dinner. The sheep has no protection under the law. However, in a republic such as ours, the wolves cannot vote to eat the sheep because the sheep is considered equal under the law. Understanding that no form of government was perfect, the Founders combined the best of both democratic and republican government. Like chocolate and peanut butter together make a Reese's Cup, the founders created a representative republic--the law rules, but those who make the laws are democratically elected within each state. Note that I say "within each state." The Founders made no provision for a "national election."

Once the founders settled the matter of representation, they had to decide whether to have a "national" government as opposed to a "federal" government. It was this debate that led in part to the formation of the Electoral College. James Madison, in *The Federalist Papers* No. 39 discusses the differences between a national government and a federal government.

A national government, writes Madison, "regards the Union as a consolidation of the States." In other words, each state gives up its sovereignty, and blends into one political body. A federal government, on the other hand, he calls "a confederacy of sovereign states." In this case, each state is its own sovereign political body. The states empower a central government to act as an agent in certain specific matters, such as defense against common enemies, the negotiation of international treaties, etc. The role of the federal government then is as a servant to the states, not a master over them. Having carefully defined the two choices, the founders established a federal, not national government.

The question of constitutional ratification was an important part of the national/federal debate. Madison illustrated the danger of making ratification a matter of popular referendum, saying "were the people regarded in this transaction as forming one nation, the will of the majority of the whole people of the United States would bind the minority."

When considering the election of a national executive, the framers applied the same principle-- federalism instead of nationalism. Those who would abolish the Electoral College ignore this. A national popular election would concentrate all power in the hands of urban centers. Without the Electoral College, the next president could be chosen by the populace of New York, California, Illinois, Ohio, Pennsylvania, and Florida, with only a smattering of other states thrown in for good measure. The Electoral College, however, ensures that Madison's vision of each state as a distinct and co-equal party becomes a reality.

Because of the Electoral College, a person in Montana, North or South Dakota, Rhode Island, or Nevada actually has a reason to get up, get dressed, and go vote. If we abolish the Electoral College, these voters will find their opinion drowned out by the mob rule that is the "popular vote", and the residents of a handful of states will choose the future presidents of this nation.

The Electoral College preserves regional identity and integrity, and protects smaller states from a tyranny imposed by large states. It is one of the few remaining bulwarks protecting us from socialism. That is why so many true liberals oppose it. Over 700 bills have been introduced to eliminate the Electoral College. 700 bills have failed. If it comes up again, here's hoping that number is 701.

THE AMERICAN FLAG

In the face of overwhelming odds and often in the face of death itself, the American flag inspires those who believe in the American dream, the American promise, the American vision.--Tom Adkins

No other inanimate object provokes the same passions in so many as the America flag. Betsy Ross created a more impressive masterpiece with a needle and some red, white, and blue threads than Michelangelo wrought on the ceiling of the Sistine Chapel. The mere sight of that tricolor banner bedecked with 13 stripes and 50 stars moves billions worldwide, but resonates especially with Americans.

Old Glory flies for all to see as the proclamation of freedom. It beckons millions around the globe to the land of opportunity. It gives hope to multitudes trapped under tyranny. It has guided the tempest tossed on rickety rafts for a treacherous journey to the Promised Land. At home it lets Americans know that all is functioning--regardless of whatever distress is currently pressing.

The American flag has led our troops into battle. It brings the security of home to valiant but lonely warriors in dreadful locations around the globe where liberty's light has been threatened. It has comforted many servicemen or women when it has been draped over one of their fallen comrades and provided the final shelter to the heroes who gave their lives defending all it represents.

Evildoers hate it. Hitler, Stalin, Pol Pot, Hussein, Mugabe, Castro, and other depraved butchers recoil in horror at its unfurling, knowing that the people they repress see it for the hope and freedom it signifies.

Back in 1989 in a (not rare enough) instance of judicial stupidity, the Supreme Court by one vote ruled that desecrating the flag is *not* a crime. Yet the American people once again proved to be wiser than the out-of-touch jurists. Efforts to deface the flag would provoke severe retaliation anywhere in the USA and almost any place else in the world where people do not live in constant fear of their brutal ruling regimes. A broad bipartisan national movement to pass a Constitutional Amendment outlawing flag desecration has been gaining momentum ever since.

Old Glory assures Americans of stability and breeds hope all over the earth, for it symbolizes a land that is good and just. Those who mess with either the flag or the country it represents must be forewarned that severe consequences await.

The quotes in this section show Americans pledging their allegiance to the flag, and some underscore the folly of the Supreme Court's inexplicable misjudgment and advocate measures to rectify the foolish edict.

We take the stars from heaven, the red from our mother country, separating it by white stripes, thus showing that we have separated from her, and the white stripes shall go down to posterity representing liberty.--George Washington

The Flag stands for everything the country stands for.--Walter Berns[1]

For me it was an especially patriotic Fourth. Just a few Days before the United States Supreme Court had overturned a lower court conviction regarding the burning of an American flag in Texas. The high court ruling had been that the perpetrator was exercising his First Amendment rights. I had thought about that ruling and something about that man's rights and my flag just didn't gel.--Ronnie Milsap[2]

The flag is our national treasure.--Marty Justis

The stars upon your banner have become nearly threefold their original number; your densely populated possessions skirt the shores of the two great oceans.--Franklin Pierce

Many a bum show has been saved by the flag.--George M. Cohan

I'm not displaying a flag on my balcony, because I already have one emblazoned on my soul.--Julia Gornin[3]

The United States Supreme Court has ruled that it is legal to burn the American flag, but that it is illegal to open or close school graduation ceremonies with a prayer. Apparently, it believes that the expression of hate is protected speech, but that in school, at least, the expression of faith should be banned.--Bret Schundler

I see that old flagpole still stands. Have your troops hoist the colors to its peak, and let no enemy ever haul them down.--Douglas MacArthur

Our flag is our national ensign, pure and simple, behold it! Listen to it! Every star has a tongue, every stripe is articulate.--Robert C. Winthrop

You can't appreciate home till you've left it, money till it's spent, your wife until she's joined a woman's club, nor Old Glory till you see it hanging on a broomstick on a shanty of a consul in a foreign town.--O. Henry

One flag, one land, one heart, one hand, One Nation evermore!
--Oliver Wendell Holmes

In my considered judgment, sanctioning the public desecration of the flag will tarnish its value – both for those who cherish the ideals for which it waves and for those who desire to don the robes of martyrdom by burning it. That tarnish is not justified by the trivial burden on free expression occasioned by requiring that an available, alternative mode of expression — including uttering words critical of the flag.--John Paul Stevens dissenting in the ill-decided flag-burning ruling

Burning a flag is not speech and should not fall under First Amendment protection.--Robert Bork

The flag of the United States of America, Old Glory, the Stars and Stripes, waved itself into my heart at an early age. It stood quietly at the front of the little Baptist church in Cotton Valley, Louisiana where it represented a second pillar in my life--that of country.--Stan Tiner

I regard the legal protection of our flag as an absolute necessity and a matter of critical importance to our nation.--Norman Schwarzkopf

The flag speaks--the only inanimate object that speaks. It says what it is and what it stands for. When draped on a coffin it says: "Herein is someone honorably dead."--Jim Burt

I believe that the States and the Federal Government do have power to protect the flag from acts of desecration and disgrace.--Earl Warren

I have loved but one flag and I cannot share that devotion and give affection to the mongrel banner invented for a league.
--Henry Cabot Lodge

The raising of that flag on Suribachi means a Marine Corps for the next 500 years.--James Forrestal

It was leadership here at home that gave us strong American influence abroad, and the collapse of imperial Communism. Great nations have responsibilities to lead, and we should always be cautious of those who would lower our profile, because they might just wind up lowering our flag.--Ronald Reagan

There is something about that (Lincoln Memorial) that forbids its desecration, and because it too causes us to remember the same ought to be true of the flag.--Walter Berns[4]

We have a long way to go to restore our foundation of "goodness," and protecting our flag would be a step in the right direction.
--Daniel S. Wheeler

The flag is qualitatively different than any other symbol we have in this country. It represents things that are uncommonly powerful, both intellectually and emotionally--love of country, the country itself, patriotism, and the sacrifices that have been made of behalf of our nation for generations.--Adrian Cronauer

I, for one, support a constitutional amendment to restore protection to our national flag, and I do so not in deference to political expediency, but because I believe it is the right thing to do and have for a long time. Our national flag has come to hold a unique position in our society as the most important and universally recognized symbol that unites us as a nation. No other symbol crosses the political, cultural, and ideological patchwork that makes up this great nation and binds us as a whole.--Diane Feinstein

It should be borne in mind that such great champions of civil liberty and free expression as Hugo Black and Earl Warren, when they served on the Supreme Court, made clear their beliefs that flag desecration was not protected by the First Amendment.--Stephen B. Presser

I didn't mind waving the flag a little bit.--Kelsey Grammer

Sure I wave the American flag. Do you know a better flag to wave? --John Wayne

That flag unites Americans as no symbol can.--Max Cleland

In 1862, a flag desecrator...was actually hanged in New Orleans. No record was found of First Amendment objections to the hanging.--D.J. Connolly

Burning the flag is wrong, but what it teaches is worse, it teaches that the outrageous conduct of a minority is more important than the will of the majority. It teaches that our laws need not reflect our values; and it teaches disrespect for the values embedded in our Constitution as embodied by our flag. The Constitution is too important to be left to the Courts and so is the flag. They both belong to the people and it is time for this body (Congress) to let the people decide.--Patrick Brady

This flag means more than association and reward. It is the symbol of our national unity, our national endeavor, our national aspiration. It tells you of the struggle for independence, of union preserved, of liberty and union one and inseparable, of the sacrifices of brave men and women to whom the ideals and honor of this nation have been dearer than life.--Charles Evans Hughes

The flag remains the single, preeminent connection among all Americans. --Norman Schwarzkopf

I want the people of all the earth to see in the American flag the symbol of a Government which intends no oppression at home and no aggression abroad, which in the spirit of a common brotherhood provides assistance in time of distress.--Calvin Coolidge

This flag which we honor and under which we serve, is the emblem of our unity, our power and our thought and purpose as a nation. It has no other character than that which we give it from generation to generation. The choices are ours. It floats in majestic silence above the hosts that execute choices, whether in peace or in war. And yet, though silent, it speaks to us, speaks to us of the past, of the men and women who went before us and of the records they wrote upon it. We celebrate the day of its birth, and from its birth until now it has witnessed a great history, has floated on high the symbol of great events, or a great plan of life worked out by a great people.
--Woodrow Wilson

One of the men stooped to his knees, unscrewed a cap to a can of lighter fluid and soaked the American flag with it. We all watched dumbstruck as the man pulled out a match and tried to light the American flag to burn it. To the astonishment of the protesters, the fans and those of us on the field, all-star outfielder Rick Monday ran at the protesters, grabbed the burning flag and ran toward the dugout as I screamed at the protesters from the third base coaching box. The fans immediately got on their feet to recognize Monday's heroic act, and without any prompting that I can remember, the whole crowd stood and began to fill the stadium with an impromptu rendition of "God Bless America"...Today, the flag-burning incident is still shown in highlights, and everyone who saw the incident then and now knows the protesters were doing something terrible, offensive and wrong.--Tommy Lasorda

Mary Jane, this is my ship's Flag, 'Old Glory.' It has been my constant companion. I love it as a mother loves her child. Cherish it as I have cherished it.--William Driver who had coined the nickname "Old Glory," to his daughter on his deathbed

Why are *The New York Times* and Senator Ted Kennedy so opposed to making it a federal crime to intentionally desecrate the U.S. flag? For more than 200 years, that was the law of the land. In 1989, the U.S. Supreme Court held by a vote of 5 to 4 that desecrating the flag was protected by the First Amendment as a form of free speech. The only way to overcome that Supreme Court decision is by the adoption of a Constitutional amendment, which would let the people decide. If there is a vote, I will vote to restore what had been the law.--Ed Koch

Consistently, the overwhelming majority of Americans have supported flag protection. Consistently, lopsided majorities in Congress have supported it too. In 1989, the House of Representatives voted 371-43 and the Senate 91-9 in favor of legislation to protect the flag. Since that route was definitively blocked by a narrow vote on the Supreme Court in 1990, over two-thirds of the House and nearly two-thirds of the Senate have supported a constitutional amendment to correct the Court's mistake and, so, permit the majority to rule on this specific question. Up to 80 percent of the American people have consistently supported the amendment. --Richard Parker

I am proud to lend my voice to those of a vast majority of Americans who support returning legal protections for the flag. The flag protection constitutional amendment is the only means of returning to the people the right to protect their flag.--Norman Schwartzkopf

Let us never forget that in honoring our flag, we honor the American men and women who have courageously fought and died for it over the last 200 years--patriots who set an ideal above any consideration of self and who suffered for it the greatest hardships. Our flag flies free today because of their sacrifice.--Ronald Reagan

It is difficult to overstate the power of the American Flag. The red, white and blue banner commands respect from whatever parapet it flies. Certain agenda-driven voices scurrilously cite any instance of governmental abuse to allege that it represents oppression and imperialism, and one group regularly singled out as "victims" of American colonialism is the American Indian. While noisy self-appointed spokespeople regularly shout this invective, the following passage penetratingly belies that mendacious mantra. David Yeagley is a patriotic American of Comanche descent and his dynamic prose will reverberate with millions of Americans of all nationalities. He engrossingly captures just how the affection for the Flag runs deeply through Americans-- including some who have valid grievances with a government that has not always lived up to the promises it has made or the ideals that Old Glory symbolizes. Human flaws will always exist, but so will the truth and goodness that the American Flag represents.

This essay first appeared online in Front Page Magazine on April 21, 2004 and is available at (http://www.frontpagemag.com/Articles/Read Article.asp?ID=13051.)

The Indians' Real Mascot: The Flag
by David Yeagley

Leftist Indian leaders famously condemn the use of Indians as school mascots, but the truth is, Indians use mascots, too. No, I'm not talking about Indian schools that have logos like "Warriors," "Chiefs," or "Indians." I mean the real mascot all Indians use: the American Flag.

Indians use the American Flag in precisely the same way that American schools use the image of the Indian. It's all about strength. The human heart enshrines emblems of strength.

It happens at very Indian powwow. The evening begins with a grand entry of all the dancers into the arena. The color guard leads with the eagle staff and the American Flag, together with a state flag, military flags, and whatever other flags are appropriate for the occasion.

Then there is a special Flag song. This is the moment the American Flag is honored by American Indians--in the way only Indians can do it.

It happened at a powwow at Oklahoma City University, March 27th. The emcee reminded everyone that we honor the flag of "this great country," and he directed everyone to the huge flag hanging from the west ceiling of the gymnasium where we were. Everyone turned toward the flag, and the singers began.

It is a solemn sound, the flag song. Slow, majestic, and powerful. Everyone knows it. Everyone respects it.

I understand why Indians honor the American Flag: It is our mascot! It is the token of the great power, the great strength--the strength that is our great White Father, who was greater than us. We don't admit it openly, but this is exactly what we are doing with the flag song.

No, it's not the American government, or American politics, or American society that we honor. It is the deep power, the grand nobility of greatness itself. Indians know and feel this in the American Flag. It's not the political parties we value. It's certainly not the justice system, or capitalism, or the pollution of earth. It is not the destruction of natural beauty, the languishing of our people under government theft and abuse of our resources. It is the glory of strength itself we see in the flag. We feel the power. That's all. The raw strength.

Indians recognize strength. It is *po-haw-cut*, as the Comanche would say: Medicine. Power. It is America. We sing and dance to America. We honor America's strength in every flag song at every powwow. I can scarcely describe it to a non-Indian.

Indians don't say it in words, yet it's there, deep within us. We have a thing for that American Flag. Not only do we honor it with prayerful song, we wear it! American Flag themes have been woven into our dance regalia for decades. Indians wear the flag in dance, in our cultural celebrations. It fascinates us. It is a sacred thing to us, not an article of daily dress.

And when Americans dress up like Indians, and use Indian images for their school teams, it's really the same intuition. Most Americans have a deep appreciation for the awesome Indian warrior. He represents something very powerful to them--a natural strength, even savagery, which is dear to the heart of most every man. It's a macho thing. It's a warrior thing.

The professional protesters who decry Indian mascots are not warriors at all. Their psychological theory that Indian mascots degrade Indians shows little understanding of Indians or mascots. Many professional protesters have never really fought anything, never won anything, and really never lost anything. Therefore, they don't know the real dynamic of the warrior experience. They don't know what a mascot is. If they think Indian mascots are bad, they shouldn't pledge allegiance to the American Flag.

"I don't do flag songs for the American Flag," an Indian recently wrote me. "I do songs for the eagle feather, for the Comanche flag and for the flags of other native nations. It is the same reason I haven't recited the Pledge of Allegiance to the US flag for the last 20 years. That would be the equivalent of a Jew saluting the swastika."

Wrong!

The America government did not believe Indians should be annihilated. America even left us land for our "nations." They declared us citizens in 1924. The U.S. government still recognizes the treaties it made with us. I'll do the flag song. And most Indians, in our heathenish way, offer the purest affection there is for Old Glory. We know its power. And grandeur.

RELIGION

Of all the dispositions and habits which lead to political prosperity, religion and morality are indispensable supports. It is impossible to rightly govern the world without God.
--George Washington

Religion may not initially seem a likely topic for inclusion in a book of patriotic quotes, but in compiling the statements for this work, one theme overwhelmed all others. Religious references are found in more of the quotations than any other subject matter. This section required the most aggressive editing due to the volume of applicable lines, and readers will notice that many other sections of the book feature items that just as easily could have been placed in this chapter.

From the nation's Founding right up right up through the post-September 11th era a healthy dose of religiosity has typified America. Recent times may provoke more officious challenges and force cautious politicos to stifle their expressions somewhat, but the tangible devotion to God that permeates America still comes through amply.

Any book of patriotic quotes needs a chapter of this nature, but to fully capture the importance Americans have placed on their faith, the section would need to be considerably longer than what this collection affords.

The Founding Fathers routinely and unabashedly invoked God's succor in their often fractious but ultimately successful efforts to cobble together the new nation. Abraham Lincoln blamed sinfulness for the Civil War and implored his fellow citizens to pray for its successful outcome. Franklin Delano Roosevelt publicly endorsed Christian precepts throughout the dark days of World War II, and nearly every other president shared a strong religious conviction and sincerely urged Americans to pray when times of great turmoil arose. Presidents are not atypical in this regard. Other leaders throughout American history from Benjamin Franklin to Albert Einstein from Patrick Henry to Douglas MacArthur have been people of faith too.

Probably every soldier from the Revolutionary War right

through the current War on Terror has turned to God for courage, stamina, and solace. America is a country with no official religion, but many observers agree that it is probably the most religious nation on earth.

This reality does not sit well with a pushy group of extremists who think that the country's most overriding precept is an impenetrable "separation of church and state." That phrase appears nowhere in the Constitution nor any official document. Thomas Jefferson used it once in a personal letter--not exactly an instrument that carries persuasive sanction.

Yet somehow the notion that faith has a role in society has become anathema in certain circles. To many movers and shakers religious beliefs must be relegated to the shadows, and those who dare allow them to inform their actions must be viewed with suspicion. Such discrimination stands in stark contrast to the views of most of the Founders, conflicts with ideals that prevailed for most of America's history, and contradicts the beliefs of most Americans today.

Had that view abounded throughout our history people like John Jay, John Adams, Ulysses S. Grant, Harriet Beecher Stowe, Martin Luther King, Jr. and John Kennedy likely would have been barred from their influential positions. Most of the abolitionists would have been dismissed as fanatics!

The phrases included here do not exactly suggest that the speakers thought God had no place in American society. Obviously no serious voice ever called for the establishment of a theocracy or even a national religion in America, and somehow, for most of our history, the population easily understood that utterances such as these were not threatening. Sentiments of a religious nature undoubtedly powerfully aided the nascent country as it assumed its sovereignty and guided it through an often stormy history that saw wars, unrest, and countless other difficulties. Fortunately, today, most decent Americans agree with the pronouncements presented below that citizens infused with religious virtues are assets--or even necessities--to a free society and should never be silenced or denigrated.

I am sure that never was a people, who had more reason to acknowledge a Divine interposition in their affairs, than those of the United States; and I should be pained to believe that they have forgotten that Agency, which was so often manifested during our Revolution, or that they failed to consider the omnipotence of that God who is alone able to protect them.--George Washington

The longer I live, the more convincing proofs I see of this truth-- that God governs in the affairs of men. And if a sparrow cannot fall to the ground without His notice, is it probable that an empire can rise without His aid?--Benjamin Franklin

Judeo-Christian roots support our luscious American tree. --Doug Giles[1]

Nor should I forget to mention here that the last act of Congress ever signed by President Lincoln was one requiring that the motto, in which he sincerely believed, "In God We Trust," should hereafter be inscribed upon all our national coin.--Schuyler Colfax

Can the liberties of a nation be thought secure when we have removed their only firm basis, a conviction in the minds of the people that these liberties are a gift of God?--Thomas Jefferson

We will win our freedom because the sacred heritage of our nation and the eternal will of God are embodied in our echoing demands. --Martin Luther King, Jr.

It is no longer enough that we pray that God may be with us on our side. We must learn to pray that we may be on God's side. --Wernher von Braun

Happiness and moral duty are inseparably connected. --George Washington

The Ten Commandments are not the laws. They are THE LAW. Man has made 32 million laws since the Commandments were handed down to Moses on Mount Sinai more than three thousand years ago, but he has never improved on God's law. The Ten Commandments are the principles by which man may live with God and man may live with man. They are the expressions of the mind of God for His creatures. They are the charter and guide of human liberty, for there can be no liberty without the law.
--Cecil B. DeMille

The sacred rights of mankind are not to be rummaged for among old parchments or musty records. They are written, as with a sunbeam, in the whole volume of human nature, by the hand of Divinity itself, and can never be erased or obscured by mortal power.--Alexander Hamilton

The authors of our Declaration of Independence recognized the Creator Himself has given human beings an inalienable right to life, liberty, and the pursuit of happiness, though of course the exercise of these rights has to be regulated with regard to the common good.--Avery Cardinal Dulles[2]

Let us raise a standard to which the wise and honest can repair; the rest is in the hands of God.--George Washington

We cannot read the history of our rise and development as a nation, without reckoning with the place the Bible has occupied in shaping the advances of the Republic.--Franklin Delano Roosevelt

And let us not trust to human effort alone, but humbly acknowledging the power and goodness of Almighty God, who presides over the destiny of nations, and who has at all times been revealed in our country's history, let us invoke His aid and His blessings upon our labors.--Grover Cleveland

Muslim organizations need to think hard about how they can help correct the distorted image of Islam that many Americans, including many people of good will, now hold. Merely blaming the misperception of others for one's plight is not enough.
--Mohammed Ayoob

Americans need to get past the image of anthrax lodged in their lungs. In fact what we've been infected by is the media's message that the world has spun out of control. The antidote is Torah, with its fundamental affirmation that the world is never out of control.
--Rabbi Daniel Lapin[3]

We shall not fight alone. God presides over the destinies of nations, and will raise up friends for us. The battle is not to the strong alone; it is to the vigilant, the active, the brave.--Patrick Henry

May it be among the dispensations of His providence to bless our beloved country with honors and with length of days. May her ways be ways of pleasantness and all her paths be peace.
--Martin Van Buren

In France I had almost always seen the spirit of religion and the spirit of freedom marching in opposite directions. But in America I found they were intimately united and that they reigned in common over the same country.--Alexis de Tocqueville

Rebellion to tyrants is obedience to God.– William Penn

We have forgotten the gracious Hand which preserved us in peace, and multiplied and enriched and strengthened us; and we have vainly imagined, in the deceitfulness of our hearts, that all these blessings were produced by some superior wisdom and virtue of our own.--Abraham Lincoln.

Providence has showered on this favored land blessings without number, and has chosen you as the guardians of freedom, to preserve it for the benefit of the human race. May He who holds in His hands the destinies of nations make you worthy of the favors He has bestowed and enable you, with pure hearts and pure hands and sleepless vigilance, to guard and defend to the end of time the great charge He has committed to your keeping.--Andrew Jackson

Relying on the aid to be derived from the other departments of the Government, I enter on the trust to which I have been called by the suffrages of my fellow-citizens with my fervent prayers to the Almighty that He will be graciously pleased to continue to us that protection which He has already so conspicuously displayed in our favor.--James Monroe

Sound morals, religious liberty, and a just sense of religious responsibility are essentially connected with all true and lasting happiness; and to that Good Being who has blessed us by the gifts of civil and religious freedom, who watched over and prospered the labors of our fathers and has hitherto preserved to us institutions far exceeding in excellence those of any other people, let us unite in fervently commending every interest of our beloved country in all future time.--William Henry Harrison

God is going to reveal to us things He never revealed before if we put our hands in His.--George Washington Carver

If men of wisdom and knowledge, of moderation and temperance, of patience, fortitude and perseverance, of sobriety, and true republican simplicity of manners, of zeal for the honor of the Supreme Being and the welfare of the commonwealth; if men possessed of these other excellent qualities are chosen to fill the seats of government, we may expect that our affairs will rest on a solid and permanent foundation.--Samuel Adams

The worship of God is a duty; the hearing and reading of sermons may be useful; but, if men rest in hearing and praying, as too many do, it is as if a tree should value itself on being watered and putting forth leaves, though it never produce any fruit.--Benjamin Franklin

All are free to believe or not believe, all are free to practice a faith or not, but those who believe must be free to speak of and act on their belief, to apply moral teaching to public questions.--Ronald Reagan

In this way we are reaffirming the transcendence of religious faith in America's heritage and future; in this way we shall constantly strengthen those spiritual weapons which forever will be our country's most powerful resource in peace and war.--Dwight D. Eisenhower on why he supported adding the phrase "under God" to the Pledge of Allegiance.

Since I was a small boy, two states have been added to our country, and two words have been added to the Pledge of Allegiance: "under God." Wouldn't it be a pity if someone said that is a prayer, and that would be eliminated from schools, too?--Red Skelton in a disturbingly prescient statement nearly 40 years ago

Only a virtuous people are capable of freedom. As nations become corrupt and vicious, they have more need of masters. --Benjamin Franklin

Good government generally begins in the family, and if the moral character of a people degenerate, their political character must soon follow.--Elias Boudinot

All the miseries and ills which men suffer from--vice, crime, ambition, injustice, oppression, slavery, and war--proceed from their despising or neglecting the precepts contained in the Bible. --Noah Webster

May the children of the stock of Abraham who dwell in this land continue to merit and enjoy the good will of the other inhabitants — while every one shall sit in safety under his own vine and fig tree and there shall be none to make him afraid.--George Washington in a letter to the Hebrew Congregation of Newport, Rhode Island in 1790

The soldier, above all other men, is required to practice the greatest act of religious training--sacrifice.--Douglas MacArthur

No government is respectable which is not just. Without unspotted purity of public faith, without sacred public principle, fidelity, and honor, no machinery of laws, can give dignity to political society. --Daniel Webster

I do benefits for all religions--I'd hate to blow the hereafter on a technicality.--Bob Hope

We are a religious people and our institutions presuppose a Supreme Being.--William O. Douglas

We have staked the future of all of our political institutions upon the capacity of mankind for self-government, upon the capacity of each and all of us to govern ourselves, to control ourselves, to sustain ourselves according to the Ten Commandments. --James Madison

A nation of well-informed men, who have been taught to know and prize the rights which God has given them, cannot be enslaved. --Benjamin Franklin

He that does good for good's sake seeks neither paradise nor reward, but he is sure of both in the end.--William Penn

If we ever forget that we are One Nation Under God, then we will be a Nation gone under.--Ronald Reagan

The only foundation of a free constitution is pure virtue.
--John Adams

The rabbi of the Jews locked in the arms of two ministers of the Gospel was a most delightful sight. There could not have been a more happy emblem.--Benjamin Rush

I have fought against the people of the North because I believed they were seeking to wrest from the South dearest rights. But I have never cherished toward them bitter or vindictive feelings, and have never seen the day when I did not pray for them.
--Robert E. Lee

Much to be regretted indeed would it be, were we to neglect the means and to depart from the road which Providence has pointed us to so plainly; I cannot believe it will ever come to pass.
--George Washington

There never have been pogroms in America; there never have been respectable anti-Semitic political parties in America; and there never have been any federal laws curtailing Jewish opportunities in America...In no Christian country has anti-Semitism been weaker than it has been in the United States.--Leonard Dinnerstein[4]

It is part of our heritage that the benefits of being free, enjoyed by all Americans, were set up by God, intended for all people. Bondage is not of God, and it is not right that any man should be in bondage at any time, in any way.--Chief Warrant Officer Paul Holton who via the Internet has arranged the shipment of more than 1,600 aid packages to Iraq's needy citizens.

I deem the present occasion sufficiently important and solemn to justify me in expressing to my fellow citizens a profound reverence for the Christian religion, and a thorough conviction that sound morals, religious liberty, and a just sense of religious responsibility are essentially connected with all true and lasting happiness.
--William Henry Harrison

Should not the Bible regain the place it once held as a school book? Its morals are pure, its examples captivating and noble.
--Fisher Ames

To obtain religious, as well as civil, liberty I entered zealously into the Revolution, and observing the Christian religion divided into many sects, I founded the hope that no one would be so predominant as to become the religion of the State. That hope was thus early entertained, because all of them joined in the same cause, with few exceptions of individuals. God grant that this religious liberty may be preserved in these States, to the end of time, and that all believing in the religion of Christ may practice the leading principle of charity, the basis of every virtue.--Charles Carroll

It is time now for Muslims to take back their faith and identify those who are not part of Islam and have lost their moral compass. Their martyrdom is fabricated under the guidance of principles that are not Islamic. To suggest even one circumstance of justification is to violate the principle of God.--M. Zuhdi Jasser

It is the duty of all Nations to acknowledge the providence of Almighty God, to obey his will, to be grateful for his benefits, and humbly to implore his protection and favors.
--George Washington

I like to trust that the God of battles has this Republic in His care.
--Whittaker Chambers

 Patriotism, which is a virtue for people of all faiths, requires that we fight, ethically and nonviolently, for what we believe.
--Archbishop Charles Chaput

The commander Rick Husband stopped before exiting, turned to his crew, and the seven embraced as one: Jew, Hindu, Christian together, and Rick led them in prayer.--Bob Cabana, Space Shuttle Columbia's Flight Crew Operations Chief[5]

Let the pulpit resound with the doctrine and sentiments of religious liberty.--John Adams

Those who would oppose the phrase, "under God" are more in the camp of those religious tyrannies they point to in supposed fear. For, without God, anything is possible by the hand of man.
--Laura Schlessinger[6]

It cannot be emphasized too strongly or too often that this great nation was founded, not by religionists, but by Christians; not on religions, but on the gospel of Jesus Christ. For this very reason peoples of other faiths have been afforded asylum, prosperity, and freedom of worship.--Patrick Henry

Should Moses have told the children of Israel to live in slavery under the pharaohs? Should Christ have refused the cross? Should the patriots of Concord Bridge have thrown down their guns and refused to fire the shot heard 'round the world? The martyrs of history were not fools, and our honored dead who gave their lives to stop the advance of the nazis didn't die in vain!--Ronald Reagan

Americans are and always have been a deeply religious people.
--Laura Ingraham[7]

America's greatness today can be attributed to our Founding Fathers who worked to establish a nation under God where everyone could pray and worship freely as they believed.
--Captain Sung-Joo Park[8]

The same revolutionary beliefs for which our forebears fought are still at issue around the globe--the belief that the rights of man come not from the generosity of the state but from the hand of God.
--John F. Kennedy

If it were within my personal power to help to return this nation to its rightful place by placing God back in the classroom, I would do it.--William J. Murray, son of infamous atheist Madelyn O'Hare[9]

I am well aware of the toil and blood and treasure, that it will cost us to maintain this Declaration, and support and defend these States.--Yet through all the gloom I can see the rays of ravishing Light and Glory. I can see that the end is more than worth all the means. And that posterity will triumph in that day's transaction, even although we should rue it, which I trust in God we shall not.
--John Adams[10]

History fails to record a single precedent in which nations subject to moral decay have not passed into political and economic decline. There has been either a spiritual awakening to overcome the moral lapse, or a progressive deterioration leading to ultimate national disaster.--Douglas MacArthur

Man will ultimately be governed by God or by tyrants.
--Benjamin Franklin

The propitious smiles of Heaven can never be expected on a nation that disregards the eternal rules of order and right which Heaven itself has ordained.--George Washington

One can hardly respect a system of education that would leave a student wholly ignorant of the currents of religious thought that moved the world.--Robert H. Jackson

My advice to Sunday schools, no matter what their denomination, is: Hold fast to the Bible as the sheet anchor of your liberties; write its precepts in your hearts, and practice them in your lives. To the influence of this Book are we indebted for all the progress made in true civilization, and to this must we look as our guide in the future. "Righteousness exalteth a nation; but sin is a reproach to any people."--Ulysses S. Grant

Our Founders believed that we have an inalienable right to conceive of God as we choose, and to teach our children our religious values.--Bret Schundler

I believe in God and I trust myself in his Hands.--James Garfield

In 1776, American Independence was declared and a revolution effected, not only in political affairs but also in those relating to Religion. For while the thirteen provinces of North America rejected the yoke of England, they proclaimed, at the same time, freedom of conscience and the right of worshipping the Almighty according to the spirit of the religion to which each one should belong.--Bishop John Carroll

I see America in the crimson light of a rising sun fresh from the burning, creative hand of God.--Carl Sandburg

America has remained silent too long. God-fearing people have remained silent too long. We must lift our voices united in a humble prayer to God for guidance and the strength and courage to sustain us throughout whatever the future may hold.--Beth Chapman

Throughout his papacy Pope John Paul II displayed both a broad knowledge of and a healthy respect for American history. He often spoke or wrote reverently about the Declaration of Independence and repeatedly invoked the Founding Fathers and other American legends in his writings and speeches. Following are excerpted remarks he delivered upon receiving then-newly appointed United States Ambassador to the Vatican Lindy Boggs on December 16, 1997. His comments highlight not only his familiarity with the American mission but his belief in the vitally important role that the United States plays worldwide. He references specific examples to accentuate the religious nature of America, and the mere fact that one of the most esteemed spiritual leaders in world history afforded such affection to the American experiment illumines the prominence Americans have bestowed upon religion throughout our history.

Remarks of Pope John Paul II upon receiving United States Ambassador to the Vatican Lindy Boggs, December 16, 1997

You represent a nation which plays a crucial role in world events today. The United States carries a weighty and far-reaching responsibility, not only for the well-being of its own people, but for the development and destiny of peoples throughout the world. With a deep sense of participation in the joys and hopes, the sorrows, anxieties, and aspirations of the entire human family, the Holy See is a willing partner in every effort to build a world of genuine peace and justice for all.

The Founding Fathers of the United States asserted their claim to freedom and independence on the basis of certain "self-evident" truths about the human person: truths which could be discerned in human nature, built into it by "nature's God." Thus they meant to bring into being, not just an independent territory, but a great experiment in what George

Washington called "ordered liberty" an experiment in which men and women would enjoy equality of rights and opportunities in "the pursuit of happiness" and in service to the common good. Reading the founding documents of the United States, one has to be impressed by the concept of freedom they enshrine: a freedom designed to enable people to fulfill their duties and responsibilities toward the family and toward the common good of the community. Their authors clearly understood that there could be no true freedom without moral responsibility and accountability, and no happiness without respect and support for the natural units or groupings through which people exist, develop, and seek the higher purposes of life in concert with others.

The American democratic experiment has been successful in many ways. Millions of people around the world look to the United States as a model, in their search for freedom, dignity, and prosperity. But the continuing success of American democracy depends on the degree to which each new generation, native-born and immigrant, make its own the moral truths on which the Founding Fathers staked the future of your Republic. Their commitment to build a free society "with liberty and justice for all" must be constantly renewed if the United States is to fulfill the destiny to which the Founders pledged their "lives...fortunes...and sacred honor."

Respect for religious conviction played no small part in the birth and early development of the United States. Thus John Dickinson, chairman of the Committee for the Declaration of Independence, said in 1776: "Our liberties do not come from charters; for these are only the declaration of pre-existing rights. They do not depend on parchments or seals; but come from the King of Kings and the Lord of all the earth." Indeed it may be asked whether the American democratic experiment would have been possible, or how well it will succeed in the future, without a deeply rooted vision of Divine Providence over the individual and over the fate of nations.

As the Year 2000 draws near and Christians prepare to celebrate the bi-millennium of the birth of Christ, I have appealed for a serious examination of conscience regarding the shadows which darken our times. Nations and States too can make this a time of reflection on the spiritual and moral conditions of their success in promoting the integral good of their people. It would truly be a sad thing if the religious and moral convictions upon which the American experiment was founded could now somehow be considered a danger to free society, such that those who would bring these convictions to bear upon your nation's public life would be denied a voice in debating and resolving issues of public policy. The original separation of Church and State in the United States was certainly not an effort to ban all religious conviction from the public sphere, a kind of banishment of God from civil society. Indeed, the vast majority of Americans, regardless of their religious persuasion, are convinced that religious conviction and religiously informed moral argument have a vital role in public life.

No expression of today's commitment to liberty and justice for all can be more basic than the protection afforded to those in society who are most vulnerable. The United States of America was founded on the conviction that an inalienable right to life was a self-evident moral truth, fidelity to which was a primary criterion of social justice. The moral history of your country is the story of your people's efforts to widen the circle of inclusion in society, so that all Americans might enjoy the protection of law, participate in the responsibilities of citizenship, and have the opportunity to make a contribution to the common good. Whenever a certain category of people--the unborn or the sick and old--are excluded from that protection, a deadly anarchy subverts the original understanding of justice. The credibility of the United States will depend more and more on its promotion of a genuine culture of life, and on a renewed commitment to building a world in which the weakest and most vulnerable are welcomed and protected.

As they have done throughout your country's history, the Catholic people in the United States will continue to make an important contribution to the development of American culture and society. The recently completed Special Assembly of the Synod of Bishops for America has highlighted the range and variety of activity which Catholics, out of commitment to Christ, undertake for the betterment of society. May this transforming and elevating work continue to flourish for the good of individuals, the strengthening of families, and the benefit of the American people as a whole.

These reflections evoke a prayer: that your country will experience "a new birth of freedom," freedom grounded in truth and ordered to goodness. Thus will the American people be able to harness their boundless spiritual energy in service of the genuine good of all humanity. Be assured that the various Offices of the Holy See will be ready to assist you in the fulfillment of your mission. Upon the people of the United States of America I cordially invoke abundant divine blessings.

THANKSGIVING

It would be an insult to God to be this blessed and not realize it.--Dolly Parton[1]

Perhaps Thanksgiving is the quintessential American holiday. For a people as fortunate as we are, setting aside a day to express gratitude is more than fitting. It is almost a natural reaction for residents of the greatest nation on earth. A single day somehow seems insufficient to commemorate all the riches we automatically receive by our status as Americans. Whether we are American as our birthright or were adopted via immigration we have something that is the envy of the world--United States citizenship. With such abundant blessings and unlimited opportunities all around us it is only fitting to designate a special day to stop and appreciate them and afford the celebration such prestige.

Even the origins of Thanksgiving--tracing back a century before the United States was incorporated--show the special aura of our land. America's earliest inhabitants knew they were in a beatific place. The Melting Pot started to simmer before the country even came into being when the native dwellers (Indians) welcomed the strangers (Pilgrims) from England. There is an overtly religious element to Thanksgiving-- even if today's radical secularists try to obfuscate that fact. The Pilgrims and the Indians knew to thank God for their plenty, and so have all wise Americans from that day forward, because the gifts God has bestowed upon our land have only generously multiplied since that first festival in Plymouth, Massachusetts.

Many Thanksgiving traditions have been added since November 29, 1621 when the inhabitants of what would later become America first marked the holiday. There was no such thing as American football in the seventeenth century. Rowland Macy had yet to open a store so there was no annual parade and no kickoff to the as-yet-unthought-of Christmas shopping season. But prominent facets remain extant from that first feast. Most of us gourmandize ourselves that day as the Pilgrims and Indians reportedly did. We all have much for which we should be grateful, and we are still reaping the magnificent cornucopia that our hallowed land yields.

Although the need to give thanks has always existed in America, and wise citizens frequently acknowledged their good fortune the day's official status has not been constant. Although the Pilgrims and their descendants marked it regularly, the first Presidential Proclamation came in 1789 when George Washington declared a day of Thanksgiving. Sporadic recurrences came after that until 1863 when Abraham Lincoln assigned the last Thursday of November each year as Thanksgiving Day. In 1941 under Franklin Delano Roosevelt the day became fixed at the fourth Thursday in November.

Its date may have changed, and in certain years there may not have been a formally sanctioned heralding, but Americans have long been a thankful lot. With all our gifts how could we not be?

This section is a bit different in that rather than one full essay as a conclusion, five American Thanksgiving proclamations are included in their entirety after the brief quotations and abbreviated presidential declarations.

We must focus again on the family, learn to be grateful for being Americans, and recover the knowledge we once had that no nation can survive without emphasizing public moral standards.--Jesse Lee Peterson[2]

Sometimes we need to remind ourselves that thankfulness is indeed a virtue.--William Bennett

We live in dangerous times, but also in the greatest times, in the greatest country this earth has ever known. Of course, let's be happy— but also grateful.--Ben Stein[3]

It seems fitting that on the occurrence of the hundredth anniversary of our existence as a nation a grateful acknowledgment should be made to Almighty God for the protection and the bounties which He has vouchsafed to our beloved country.--Ulysses S. Grant on America's centennial

The thing I'm most grateful for at this moment is the opportunity America affords so that anyone with a little encouragement and internal drive can move onward and upward.--Zig Ziglar

We've largely forgotten the true meaning of Thanksgiving in recent years. Too many of us celebrate the day not with prayers but by gorging ourselves on turkey and football.--Linda Chavez[4]

We should all pause a moment for perspective, and give thanks for America and the American way of life; a way of life that is bound up in the Bill of Rights; a way of life that treasures those basic freedoms that we associate with happiness, like the freedom to better oneself, to determine one's own destiny, to pursue happiness on one's own terms, and most importantly, the freedom to be left alone.--Armstrong Williams[5]

Thank God we're living in a country where the sky's the limit.
--Joan Rivers

There is a calmness to a life lived in Gratitude, a quiet joy.
--Ralph Blum

Many times a day I realize how much my own life is built on the labors of my fellowmen, and how earnestly I must exert myself in order to give in return as much as I have received.--Albert Einstein

Gratitude is one of the least articulate of the emotions, especially when it is deep.--Felix Frankfurter

For precious life itself in this great nation--under God, indivisible, with liberty and justice for all--we thank thee, O Father.--Michelle Malkin[6]

Today, it is rare that we even take time to consider that America's blessings of prosperity, freedom, justice, peace and opportunity are gifts from a mighty and gracious God.--Hans Zeiger[7]

No people ought to feel greater obligations to celebrate the goodness of the Great Disposer of Events of the Destiny of Nations than the people of the United States. His kind providence originally conducted them to one of the best portions of the dwelling place allotted for the great family of the human race. He protected and cherished them under all the difficulties and trials to which they were exposed in their early days. Under His fostering care their habits, their sentiments, and their pursuits prepared them for a transition in due time to a state of independence and self-government. In the arduous struggle by which it was attained they were distinguished by multiplied tokens of His benign interposition. During the interval which succeeded He reared them into the strength and endowed them with the resources which have enabled them to assert their national rights, and to enhance their national character in another arduous conflict, which is now so happily terminated by a peace and reconciliation with those who have been our enemies.--James Madison, 1815

The civil war that so recently closed among us has not been anywhere reopened; foreign intervention has ceased to excite alarm or apprehension; intrusive pestilence has been benignly mitigated; domestic tranquility has improved, sentiments of conciliation has largely prevailed, and affections of loyalty and patriotism have been widely renewed; our fields have yielded quite abundantly, our mining industry has been richly rewarded, and we have been allowed to extend our railroad system far into the interior recesses of the country, while our commerce has resumed its customary activity in foreign seas. These great national blessings demand a national acknowledgment.
--Andrew Johnson, 1866

The year which is drawing to a close has been free from pestilence; health has prevailed throughout the land; abundant crops reward the labors of the husbandman; commerce and manufactures have successfully prosecuted their peaceful paths; the mines and forests have yielded liberally; the nation has increased in wealth and in strength; peace has prevailed, and its blessings have advanced every interest of the people in every part of the Union; harmony and fraternal intercourse restored are obliterating the marks of past conflict and estrangement; burdens have been lightened; means have been increased; civil and religious liberty are secured to every inhabitant of the land, whose soil is trod by none but freemen. It becomes a people thus favored to make acknowledgment to the Supreme Author from whom such blessings flow of their gratitude and their dependence, to render praise and thanksgiving for the same, and devoutly to implore a continuance of God's mercies.
--Ulysses S. Grant, 1869

Now, therefore, I, Rutherford B. Hayes, President of the United States, do appoint Thursday, the 27th day of November instant, as a day of national thanksgiving and prayer; and I earnestly recommend that, withdrawing themselves from secular cares and labors the people of the United States do meet together on that day in their respective places of worship, there to give thanks and praise to Almighty God for His mercies and to devoutly beseech their continuance.--Rutherford B. Hayes, 1879

The countless benefits which have showered upon us during the past twelvemonth call for our fervent gratitude and make it fitting that we should rejoice with thankfulness that the Lord in His infinite mercy has most signally favored our country and our people. Peace without and prosperity within have been vouchsafed to us, no pestilence has visited our shores, the abundant privileges of freedom which our fathers left us in their wisdom are still our increasing heritage; and if in parts of our vast domain sore affliction has visited our brethren in their forest homes, yet even this calamity has been tempered and in a manner sanctified by the generous compassion for the sufferers which has been called forth throughout our land. For all these things it is meet that the voice of the nation should go up to God in devout homage.
--Chester A. Arthur, 1881

The blessings demanding our gratitude are numerous and varied. For the peace and amity which subsist between this Republic and all the nations of the world; for the freedom from internal discord and violence; for the increasing friendship between the different sections of the land; for liberty, justice, and constitutional government; for the devotion of the people to our free institutions and their cheerful obedience to mild laws; for the constantly increasing strength of the Republic while extending its privileges to fellow-men who come to us; for the improved means of internal communication and the increased facilities of intercourse with other

nations; for the general prevailing health of the year; for the prosperity for all our industries, the liberal return for the mechanic's toil affording a market for the abundant harvests of the husbandman; for the preservation of the national faith and credit; for wise and generous provision to effect the intellectual and moral education of our youth; for the influence upon the conscience of a restraining and transforming religion, and for the joys of home--for these and for many other blessings we should give thanks.
--Chester A Arthur, 1882

A highly favored people, mindful of their dependence on the bounty of Divine Providence, should seek fitting occasion to testify gratitude and ascribe praise to Him who is the author of their many blessings. It behooves us, then, to look back with thankful hearts over the past year and bless God for His infinite mercy in vouchsafing to our land enduring peace, to our people freedom from pestilence and famine, to our husbandmen abundant harvests, and to them that labor a recompense of their toil.
--Benjamin Harrison 1889

While the American people should every day remember with praise and thanksgiving the divine goodness and mercy which have followed them since their beginning as a nation, it is fitting that one day in each year should be especially devoted to the contemplation of the blessings we have received from the hand of God and to the grateful acknowledgment of His loving kindness.
--Grover Cleveland, 1893

In remembrance of God's goodness to us during the past year, which has been so abundant. "Let us offer Him our thanksgiving and pay our vows unto the Most High." Under His watchful providence, industry has prospered, the conditions of labor have been improved, the rewards of the husbandman have been increased, and the comforts of our homes multiplied. His mighty hand has preserved peace and protected the nation. Respect for law and order has been strengthened, love of free institutions cherished, and all sections of our beloved country brought into closer bonds of fraternal regard and generous cooperation. For these great benefits it is our duty to praise the Lord in a spirit of humility and gratitude, and to offer up to Him our most earnest supplications. That we may acknowledge our obligation as a people to Him who has so graciously granted us the blessings of free government and material prosperity.--William McKinley, 1897

The skies have been for a time darkened by the cloud of war, but as we were compelled to take up the sword in the cause of humanity we are permitted to rejoice that the conflict has been of brief duration and the losses we have had to mourn, though grievous and important, have been so few, considering the great results accomplished, as to inspire us with gratitude and praise to the Lord of Hosts.--William McKinley, 1898

During this past year we have been highly blessed. No great calamities of flood or tempest or epidemic sickness have befallen us. We have lived in quietness, undisturbed by wars or rumors of war. Peace and the plenty of bounteous crops and of great industrial production animate a cheerful and resolute people to all the renewed energies of beneficent industry and material and moral progress. It is altogether fitting that we should humbly and gratefully acknowledge the divine source of these blessings.---William Howard Taft, 1909

Though we have lived in the shadow of the hard consequences of great conflict, our country has been at peace and has been able to contribute toward the maintenance and perpetuation of peace in the world. We have seen the race of mankind make gratifying progress on the way to permanent peace, toward order and restored confidence in its high destiny. For the Divine guidance which has enabled us, in growing fraternity with other peoples, to attain so much of progress; for the bounteous yield which has come to us from the resources of our soil and our industry, we owe our tribute of gratitude, and with it our acknowledgment of the duty and obligation to our own people and to the unfortunate, the suffering, the distracted of other lands. Let us in all humility acknowledge how great is our debt to the Providence which has generously dealt with us, and give devout assurance of unselfish purpose to play a helpful and ennobling part in human advancement.--Warren G. Harding, 1922

We are deeply grateful for the bounties of our soil, for the unequaled production of our mines and factories, and for all the vast resources of our beloved country, which have enabled our citizens to build a great civilization. We are thankful for the enjoyment of our personal liberties and for the loyalty of our fellow Americans.--Harry Truman, 1950

In 1863 Abraham Lincoln, the 16th President, lifted the downcast view of a war-weary Nation to see the evidence of God's bounty. He proclaimed a day of Thanksgiving to be observed by each American in his own way. President Lincoln wisely knew that a man's declaration of his gratitude to God is, in itself, an act which strengthens the thanksgiver because it renews his own realization of his relationship to his God. As thanksgiving enriches the individual it must bless his home, community and his country. It is, therefore, appropriate that we set aside such a day this year. All about us, doubts and fears threaten our faith in the principles which are the fiber of our society; we are called upon to prove their truth once again. Such challenges must be seen as opportunities for proof of these verities; such proof can only strengthen our Nation.--Richard Nixon, 1970

America and the world have changed enormously since the first Thanksgiving 353 years ago. From a tiny coastal enclave on an untamed continent, we have grown into the mightiest, freest nation in human history. A civilization whose farthest reach was once the earth's uncharted seas has now plumbed the secrets of outer space. But the fundamental meaning of Thanksgiving still remains the same. It is a time when the differences of a diverse people are forgotten and all Americans join in giving thanks to God for the blessings we share--the blessings of freedom, opportunity and abundance that make America so unique.--Gerald Ford, 1974

Two hundred years ago, the Congress of the United States issued a Thanksgiving Proclamation stating that it was "the indispensable duty of all nations" to offer both praise and supplication to God. Above all other nations of the world, America has been especially blessed and should give special thanks. We have bountiful harvests, abundant freedoms, and a strong, compassionate people. --Ronald Reagan, 1982

As we continue the Thanksgiving tradition, a tradition cherished by every generation of Americans, we reflect in a special way on the blessings of the past year. When this Nation and its coalition partners took up arms in a last-resort effort to repel aggression in the Persian Gulf, we were spared the terrible consequences of a long and protracted struggle. Indeed, the millions of people who prayed for a quick end to the fighting saw those prayers answered with a swiftness and certainty that exceeded all expectations. During the past year, we have also witnessed the demise of communism and welcomed millions of courageous people into the community of free nations.--George H.W. Bush, 1991

The excerpts from several presidential proclamations included in the Thanksgiving collection show that a sense of gratitude has been another defining characteristic of America since its inception. Many times when fear or trouble seems insurmountable, human nature has a tendency to forget just how blessed we are despite the trials we face. Wise Americans have always known that appreciative supplication to the Author of Liberty is essential--especially in times of extreme hardship. Life was not easy for the Pilgrims those first few years in an unfamiliar land, nor was it a bed of roses in the early days of the newly established Republic when even the most fervent patriots had legitimate doubts about the infant nation's chances for survival. It is hard now to comprehend the pain and anguish that must have saturated the nation during the difficult years of the Civil War. Pearl Harbor and September 11th both devastated an unwary populace and left Americans frightened and dazed. Yet even at these challenging times, there was much that was good and admirable. Adversity often brings out the best in people, and many Americans saw these struggles as occasions to give thanks for whatever good fortunes we had. The Thanksgiving Proclamations that correspond with the five events referenced above are included in their entirety below. Hopefully, they will help us all realize how many burdens America has already overcome and leave us with a sense of hope and gratefulness as we move forward.

William Bradford, 1623

Inasmuch as the great Father has given us this year an abundant harvest of Indian corn, wheat, peas, beans, squashes, and garden vegetables, and has made the forests to abound with game and the sea with fish and clams, and inasmuch as he has protected us from the ravages of the savages, has spared us from pestilence and disease, has granted us freedom to worship God according to the dictates of our own conscience.

Now I, your magistrate, do proclaim that all ye Pilgrims, with your wives and ye little ones, do gather at ye meeting house, on ye hill, between the hours of 9 and 12 in the day time, on Thursday, November 29th, of the year of our Lord one thousand six hundred and twenty-three and the third year since ye Pilgrims landed on ye Pilgrim Rock, there to listen to ye pastor and render thanksgiving to ye Almighty God for all His blessings.

George Washington, 1789

Whereas it is the duty of all Nations to acknowledge the providence of Almighty God, to obey his will, to be grateful for his benefits, and humbly to implore his protection and favor, and whereas both Houses of Congress have by their joint Committee requested me to recommend to the People of the United States a day of public thanksgiving and prayer to be observed by acknowledging with grateful hearts the many signal favors of mighty God, especially by affording them an opportunity peaceably to establish a form of government for their safety and happiness.

Now therefore I do recommend and assign Thursday the 26th day of November next to be devoted by the People of these States to the service of that great and glorious Being, who is the beneficent author of all the good that was, that is, or that will be. That we may then all unite in rendering unto him our sincere and humble thanks, for his kind care and protection of the People of this country previous to their becoming a Nation, for the signal and manifold mercies, and the favorable interpositions of his providence, which we experienced in the course and conclusion of the late war, for the great degree of tranquility, union, and plenty, which we have since enjoyed, for the peaceable and rational manner in which we have been enabled to establish constitutions of government for our safety and happiness, and particularly the national One now lately instituted, for the civil and religious liberty with which we are blessed, and the means we have of acquiring and diffusing useful knowledge and in general for all the great and various favors which He hath been pleased to confer upon us.

And also that we may then unite in most humbly offering our prayers and supplications to the great Lord and Ruler of Nations and beseech Him to pardon our national and other transgressions, to enable us all, whether in public or private stations, to perform our several and relative duties properly and punctually, to render our national government a blessing to all the People, by constantly being a government of wise, just and constitutional laws, discreetly and faithfully executed and obeyed, to protect and guide all Sovereigns and Nations (especially such as have shown kindness unto us) and to bless them with good government, peace and concord. To promote the knowledge and practice of true religion and virtue, and the increase of science among them and us, and generally to grant unto all Mankind such a degree of temporal prosperity as He alone knows to be best. Given under my hand at the City of New York the third day of October in the year of our Lord 1789.

Abraham Lincoln, 1868

The year that is drawing towards its close, has been filled with the blessings of fruitful fields and healthful skies. To these bounties, which are so constantly enjoyed that we are prone to forget the source from which they come, others have been added, which are of so extraordinary a nature, that they cannot fail to penetrate and soften even the heart which is habitually insensible to the ever watchful providence of Almighty God.

In the midst of a civil war of unequaled magnitude and severity, which has sometimes seemed to foreign states to invite and to provoke their aggression, peace has been preserved with all nations, order has been maintained, the laws have been respected and obeyed, and harmony has prevailed everywhere except in the theatre of military conflict; while that theatre has been greatly contracted by the advancing armies and navies of the Union. Needful diversions of wealth and of strength from the fields of peaceful industry to the national defense have not arrested the plough, the shuttle, or the ship; the axe has enlarged the borders of our settlements, and the mines, as well of iron and coal as of the precious metals, have yielded even more abundantly than heretofore. Population has steadily increased, notwithstanding the waste that has been made in the camp, the siege, and the battlefield; and the country, rejoicing in the consciousness of augmented strength and vigor, is permitted to expect continuance of years with large increase of freedom.

No human counsel hath devised nor hath any mortal hand worked out these great things. They are the gracious gifts of the Most High God, who, while dealing with us in anger for our sins, hath nevertheless remembered mercy. It has seemed to me fit and proper that they should be solemnly, reverently, and gratefully acknowledged as with one heart and one voice by the whole American People.

I do therefore invite my fellow citizens in every part of the United States, and also those who are at sea and those who are sojourning in foreign lands, to set apart and observe the last Thursday of November next, as a day of Thanksgiving and Praise to our beneficent Father who dwelleth in the Heavens. And I recommend to them that while offering up the ascriptions justly due to Him for such singular deliverances and blessings, they do also, with humble penitence for our national perverseness and disobedience, commend to His tender care all those who have become widows, orphans, mourners or sufferers in the lamentable civil strife in which we are unavoidably engaged, and fervently implore the interposition of the Almighty Hand to heal the wounds of the nation and to restore it as soon as may be consistent with the Divine purposes to the full enjoyment of peace, harmony, tranquility, and Union.

In testimony whereof, I have hereunto set my hand and caused the Seal of the United States to be affixed.
Done at the City of Washington, this Third day of October, in the year of our Lord one thousand eight hundred and sixty-three, and of the Independence of the United States the Eighty-eighth.

Franklin Delano Roosevelt, 1942

"It is a good thing to give thanks unto the Lord." Across the uncertain ways of space and time our hearts echo those words, for the days are with us again when, at the gathering of the harvest, we solemnly express our dependence upon Almighty God.

The final months of this year, now almost spent, find our Republic and the nations joined with it waging a battle on many fronts for the preservation of liberty.

In giving thanks for the greatest harvest in the history of our nation, we who plant and reap can well resolve that in the year to come we will do all in our power to pass that milestone; for by our labors in the fields we can share some part of the sacrifice with our brothers and sons who wear the uniform of the United States.

It is fitting that we recall now the reverent words of George Washington, "Almighty God, we make our earnest prayer that Thou wilt keep the United States in Thy holy protection," and that every American in his own way lift his voice to Heaven.

I recommend that all of us bear in mind this great Psalm:

The Lord is my shepherd; I shall not want.
He maketh me to lie down in green pastures;
He leadeth me beside the still waters.

He restoreth my soul;
He leadeth me in the paths of righteousness for
His name's sake.
Yea, though I walk through the valley of the
shadow of death,
I will fear no evil; for thou art with me;
thy rod and thy staff they comfort me.
Thou preparest a table before me in the
presence of mine enemies;
thou annointest my head with oil;
my cup runneth over.
Surely goodness and mercy shall follow
me all the days of my life; and I will dwell
in the house of the Lord forever

Inspired with faith and courage by these words, let us turn again to the work that confronts us in this time of national emergency: in the armed services and the merchant marine; in factories and offices; on farms and in the mines; on highways, railways and airways; in other places of public service to the Nation; and in our homes.

Now Therefore, I, Franklin D. Roosevelt, President of the United States of America, do hereby invite the attention of the people to the joint resolution of Congress approved December 26, 1941, which designates the fourth Thursday in November of each year as Thanksgiving Day, and I request that both Thanksgiving Day, November 26, 1942, and New Year's Day, January 1, 1943, be observed in prayer, publicly and privately. In witness whereof, I have hereunto set my hand and caused the seal of the United States of America to be affixed.

done at the City of Washington this eleventh day of November, in the year of our Lord nineteen hundred and forty-two, and of the Independence of the United States of America the one hundred and sixty-seventh.

George W. Bush, 2001

Nearly half a century ago, President Dwight Eisenhower proclaimed Thanksgiving as a time when Americans should celebrate "the plentiful yield of our soil . . . the beauty of our land . . . the preservation of those ideals of liberty and justice that form the basis of our national life, and the hope of international peace." Now, in the painful aftermath of the September 11 attacks and in the midst of our resolute war on terrorism, President Eisenhower's hopeful words point us to our collective obligation to defend the enduring principles of freedom that form the foundation of our Republic.

During these extraordinary times, we find particular assurance from our Thanksgiving tradition, which reminds us that we, as a people and individually, always have reason to hope and trust in God, despite great adversity. In 1621 in New England, the Pilgrims gave thanks to God, in whom they placed their hope, even though a bitter winter had taken many of their brethren. In the winter of 1777, General George Washington and his army, having just suffered great misfortune, stopped near Valley Forge, Pennsylvania, to give thanks to God. And there, in the throes of great difficulty, they found the hope they needed to persevere. That hope in freedom eventually inspired them to victory.

In 1789, President Washington, recollecting the countless blessings for which our new Nation should give thanks, declared the first National Day of Thanksgiving. And decades later, with the Nation embroiled in a bloody civil war, President Abraham Lincoln revived what is now an annual tradition of issuing a presidential proclamation of Thanksgiving. President Lincoln asked God to "heal the wounds of the nation and to restore it as soon as may be consistent with the Divine purposes to the full enjoyment of peace, harmony, tranquility, and Union."

As we recover from the terrible tragedies of September 11, Americans of every belief and heritage give thanks to God for the many blessings we enjoy as a free, faithful, and fair-minded land. Let us particularly give thanks for the selfless sacrifices of those who responded in service to others after the terrorist attacks, setting aside their own safety as they reached out to help their neighbors. Let us also give thanks for our leaders at every level who have planned and coordinated the myriad of responses needed to address this unprecedented national crisis. And let us give thanks for the millions of people of faith who have opened their hearts to those in need with love and prayer, bringing us a deeper unity and stronger resolve.

In thankfulness and humility, we acknowledge, especially now, our dependence on One greater than ourselves. On this day of Thanksgiving, let our thanksgiving be revealed in the compassionate support we render to our fellow citizens who are grieving unimaginable loss; and let us reach out with care to those in need of food, shelter, and words of hope. May Almighty God, who is our refuge and our strength in this time of trouble, watch over our homeland, protect us, and grant us patience, resolve, and wisdom in all that is to come.

Now Therefore, I, George W. Bush, President of the United States of America, by virtue of the authority vested in me by the Constitution and laws of the United States, do hereby proclaim Thursday, November 22, 2001, as a National Day of Thanksgiving. I encourage Americans to assemble in their homes, places of worship, or community centers to reinforce ties of family and community, express our profound thanks for the many blessings we enjoy, and reach out in true gratitude and friendship to our friends around the world.

In Witness Whereof, I have hereunto set my hand this sixteenth day of November, in the year of our Lord two thousand one, and of the Independence of the United States of America the two hundred and twenty-sixth.

Military Endnotes

1) John O'Neil, "Kerry 'loose cannon,' says ex-commander, World Net Daily, May 4, 2004. (http://www.worldnetdaily.com/news/article.asp? ARTICLE_ID=38337.)

2) Dennis Prager, "Thank God for moral violence," World Net Daily, April 30, 2002, (available at http://www.worldnetdaily.com/news/article.asp? ARTICLE_ID=27434.)

3) Karl Zinsmeister, *Boots on the Ground: A Month with the 82nd Airborne in the Battle for Iraq*, Truman Talley Books, 2003.

4) Joanne Jacobs, "Teaching tales,"Jewish World Review, March 3, 2003.

5) Christopher Ward, "Kerry no hero in eyes of Vietnam-era veteran," *the Atlanta Journal Constitution*, February 9, 2004.

6) B. G. Burkett and Glenna Whitley, *Stolen Valor*, Verity Press, Inc., 1998.

7) Ibid.

8) Gail Buckley, *American Patriots: The Story of Blacks in the Military from the Revolution to Desert Storm*, Random House, 2001.

9) Cal Thomas, "The Choice Accommodate or defeat Evil," Townhall, January 5, 2004, (available at http://www.townhall.com/columnists/cal thomas/ct20040105.shtml.)

10) Op cit., Burkett and Whitley.

11) Ibid.

12) Ibid.

13) Ibid.

14) Ibid.

15) Ibid.

16) Ibid.

17) Brenda Lee with Julie Clay, *Little Miss Dynamite: The Life and Times of Brenda Lee,* Hyperion, 2002.

18) Don Feder, "Americans again stand with muskets in hand," Jewish World Review, April 15, 2002, (available at http://www.jewishworld review.com/cols/feder041502.asp.)

19) Mark Steyn, "The cost of losing," *the Washington Times,* date not provided, (available at http://www.washtimes.com/commentary/ 20040502-103050-7501r.htm.)

20) Op. Cit., Buckley.

21) Ibid.

22) Barbara Mandrell with George Vecsey, *Get To The Heart: My Story,* Bantam Books, 1990.

23) Craige McMillan, "Why do they Hate Us?" World Net Daily, February 5, 2004 (available at http://www.worldnetdaily.com/news/article.asp? ARTICLE_ID=36954.)

Justice Endnotes

1) Susan L. Boyd, "A Document to Be Remembered for All Times," Ashbrook University Res Publica, April 1994, (available at http://www.ashbrook.org/publicat/respub/v5n1 /boyd.html.)

2) Jonah Goldberg, "Guess who's changing tune on Constitutional amendments?" Jewish World Review, March 3, 2004, (available at http://www.jewishworldreview.com/cols/ jonah030304.asp.)

3) Paul Greenberg, "Iraq goals," *The Washington Times*, date not provided, (available at http://www.washtimes.com/commentary/20040106-094000-7851r.htm.)

4) Margaret A. Hagen, *Whores of the Court: The Fraud of Psychiatric Testimony and the Rape of American Justice*, ReganBooks, 1997.

5) Mike Huckabee with John Perry, *Character is the Issue*, Broadman & Holman Publishers, 1997.

6) Alan Dershowitz, Fair Targets, Original source unknown, April 25, 2004, (available at http://www.aish.com/jewishissues/middleeast/Fair_Targets.asp)

7) Paul Craig Roberts and Lawrence M. Stratton, *The Tyranny of Good Intentions: How Prosecutors and Bureaucrats Are Trampling the Constitution in the Name of Justice*, Prima Lifestyles, 2000.

8) Lynne V. Cheney, *Telling the Truth: Why Our Culture and Our Country Have Stopped Making Sense--and What We Can Do About It*, Simon & Schuster, 1995.

9) Steven and Patti Anne McDonald with E.J. Kahn, *The Steven McDonald Story*, Dutton Adult, 1989.

10) Charles Krauthammer, "This war is also about sex," Townhall, May 7, 2004, (available at http://www.townhall.com/columnists/charles krauthammer/ck20040507.shtml.)

11) Dr. Kelly Hollowell, "Abortion and terrorism: Chillingly similar," World Net Daily, June 26, 2004, (available at http://wnd.com/news /article.asp?ARTICLE_ID=39147.)

12) Wesley Allen Riddle, "Born on the Fourth of July," original source unknown, July 4, 2004. (available at http://www.belogical.com/fourth_of_july_celebration.htm.)

13) Mark Levin, *Men in Black*, Regnery Publishing Inc., 2005.

14) Op. Cit., MacDonald.

15) Jeff Jacoby, "A little less freedom of speech," *the Boston Globe*, January 25, 2004.

Freedom Endnotes

1) Norman Podhoretz, *My Love Affair With America*, The Free Press, New York, 2000.

2) Ak'Bar Shabazz, ''Stay the course, Mr. President,' Townhall.com, March 10, 2004, (available at http://www.townhall.com/columnists/Guest Columns/printShabazz20040310.shtml.)

3) Tonya Flynt-Vega, *Hustled*, Westminster John Knox Press, Louisville, KY, 1998.

September 11 Endnotes

1) Dennis Prager, "9-11 made America better," World Net Daily, September 10, 2002, (available at http://worldnetdaily.com/news/ article.asp?ARTICLE_ID=28894.)

2) Mona Charen, "Time for courage," Townhall, September 14, 2001, (available at http://www.townhall.com/columnists/monacharen/mc 20010914.shtml.)

3) Ben Shapiro, "Idiot on Campus," Townhall, May 5, 2004, (available at http://www.townhall.com/columnists/benshapiro/bs20040505.shtml.)

4) Peggy Noonan, "What I Saw at the Devastation," *The Wall Street Journal*, September 13, 2001.

5) Don Feder, "Pacifism isn't just wrong, it's immoral," Jewish World Review, November 7, 2001, (available at http://www.jewishworldreview. com/cols/feder 110701.asp.)

6) Rabbi Noah Weinberg, "The Madness," www.aish.com, date not provided, (available at http://www.aish.com/societyWork/society /The_Madness.asp.)

7) Rear Admiral Rodney P. Rempt, U.S. Naval War College Press Release, "On Board *USS John F Kennedy* (CV 67), preparing to launch a combat strike in support of Operation Enduring Freedom," date not provided, (available at http://www.nwc.navy.mil/press/Review/2002/ spring/pf-sp2.htm.)

8) Marlon Mohammed, "U.S. Muslims Should Tolerate the Stares," *The Los Angeles Times*, September 29 2001.

9) Karl Zinsmeister, "That Insufferable Wonder," *American Enterprise*, June 2002.

10) Jeff Jacoby, "Offense, not Defense is the key to homeland security," Jewish World Review, June 17, 2002, (available at http://www.jewish worldreview.com/jeff/jacoby061702.asp.)

11) Peggy Noonan, "Time to Put the Emotions Aside," *The Wall Street Journal*, September 11, 2002.

12) Daniel Henninger, "LBJ Stands For: a) A President b) A Rap Singer," *The Wall Street Journal*, September 20, 2002.

13) J. Matt Barber, "Liberal Democrats--Tools of the Terrorist," The Conservative Voice, January 31, 2005, (available at http://www.the conservativevoice.com/articles/category.html?id=103.)

13) Barbara Olson, *The Final Days: The Last, Desperate Abuses of Power by the Clinton White House*, Regnery Publishing, Inc, 2001.

14) David Schippers, *Sellout The Inside Story of President Clinton's Impeachment*, Regnery Publishing, Inc., 2000.

Iraq's Liberation Endnotes

1) M Zuhdi Jasser, "Muslims must speak out," *Arizona Central*, April 6, 2004, (available at http://www.azcentral.com/specials/pluggedin/articles/0406jasser0406fallujah.html.)

2) Laura Schlessinger, "Schools making sissies out of our kids," World Net Daily, February 13, 2004, (available at http://www.worldnetdaily.com/news/printer-friendly.asp?ARTICLE_ID=37090.)

3) Amir Taheri, "Plunging into chaos?," Townhall, February 3, 2004, (available at http://www.townhall.com/columnists/GuestColumns/Taheri20040203.shtml0.)

4) Oriana Fallaci, *The Rage and The Pride*, Rizzoli, 2002.

5) Charles Krauthammer, "What David Kay really said," Townhall, January 30, 2004, (available at http://www.townhall.com/columnists/charleskrauthammer/ck 20040130.shtm.)

6) James Taranto, "Best of the Web Today: Soldiers as Victims," *The Wall Street Journal*, April 5, 2004, (available at http://www.opinionjournal.com/best/?id= 110004912.)

7) Ayad Rahim, "An Iraqi Thanksgiving," *The Wall Street Journal*, July 26, 2003, (available at http://www.opinionjournal.com/editorial/feature.html?id=110003801.)

8) Scott E. Rutter, "Our Finest Hour," Front Page Magazine, January 5, 2004, (available at http://www.frontpagemagazine.com/Articles/ReadArticle.asp?ID=11554.)

9) Tammy Bruce, "MoveOn Freudian Nazi Ad," Front Page Magazine, January 6, 2004, (available at http://www.frontpagemag.net/Articles/ReadArticle.asp?ID=11604.)

10) Jeff Jacoby, "Justice and Saddam Hussein," Jewish World Review, December 18, 2003, (available at http://www.jewishworldreview.com/jeff/jacoby121803.asp.)

11) Victor Davis Hanson, "The Event of the Age," *National Review*, October 24, 2003, (available at http://www.nationalreview.com/hanson/hanson 200310240838.asp.)

12) Ann Coulter, "War-torn Dems," Jewish World Review, January 30, 2003, (available at http://www.jewishworldreview.com/cols/coulter013003.asp.)

13) Helle Dale, "Food for fraud," *The Washington Times*, date not provided, (available at http://www.washtimes.com/op-ed/20040420-084523-1240r.htm.)

14) Karl Zinsmeister, *Boots on the Ground: A Month with the 82nd Airborne in the Battle for Iraq,* Truman Talley Books, 2003.

American Character Endnotes

1) Balint Vazsonyi, *America's Thirty Years War*, Regnery Publishing, Inc. 1998.

2) David McCullough, *John Adams*, Simon & Schuster, 2002.

3) Evelyn Husband with Donna Vanliere, *High Calling*, Thomas Nelson Publishers, 2003.

4) Kathleen Parker, "You say Fallujah, I say Rambo," *Orlando Sentinel*, April 2, 2004.

5) John L. Perry, "Character Counts," Newsmax.com, March 25, 2004. (available at http://www.newsmax.com/archives/articles/2004/3/25 /152145.shtml.)

American Culture Endnotes

1) Rebecca Hagelin, "Cultural terrorism," Townhall, February 4, 2004, (available at http://www.townhall.com/columnists/rebeccahagelin/rh 20040204.shtml.)

2) Michael Medved, "Can Hollywood change its ugly version of USA?," Jewish World Review, October 16, 2001, (available at http://www.jewish worldreview.com/cols/medved101601.asp.)

3) Dinesh D'Souza, *What's So Great About America?*, Regnery Publishing, Inc., 2002.

4) Lowell Ponte, "Dem-Iraq-racy," Front Page Magazine, February 13, 2004, (available at http://www.frontpagemag.com/Articles/Read Article.asp?ID=12186.)

5) Tammy Bruce, "Exposing Viacom's Indecency," Men's News Daily, February 3, 2004, (available at http://mensnewsdaily.com/archive/a-b/bruce/2004/bruce020304.htm.)

6) Ronald Radosh, *Commies: A Journey Through the Old Left, the New Left and the Leftover Left*, Encounter Books, 2001.

7) Norman Podhoretz, *My Love Affair with America*, The Free Press, 2000.

8) Suzanne Fields, "Taking aim at the arms suppliers in the culture war," Jewish World Review, March 8, 2004, (available at http://www.jewishworldreview.com/cols/fields 030804.asp.)

9) William Bennett, *The Broken Hearth: Reversing the Moral Collapse of the American Family*, WaterBrook Press, 2001.

10) Lynn Munson, *Exhibitionism: Art in an Era of Intolerance*, Ivan R. Dee, Publisher, 2000. (italics in original)

11) Tonya Flynt-Vega, *Hustled*, Westminster John Knox Press, Louisville, KY, 1998.

12) Gertrude Himmelfarb, *One Nation, Two Cultures*, Alfred A Knopf, New York, 1999.

13) Kelly Boggs, "First Person: Dad, daughter & porn puff piece," *Baptist Press*, April 16, 2004.

14) Michele Malkin, "the lost patriots of Hollywood," Townhall, June 23, 2004, (available at http://www.townhall.com/columnists/michellemalkin/printmm 20040623.shtml.)

Immigration Endnotes

1) Yakov Smirnoff, *America on Six Rubles a Day or How to Become a Capitalist Pig*, Vintage, 1987.

2) Ofelia Bayutas Mutia, "My tribute to Heroes, A grateful Immigrant," Global Influence, April 19, 2003, (available at http://www.oroquietacity. com/Foreword/MyTribute.html.)

3) Barbara Simpson, "Never Ever Forget," World Net Daily, May 31, 2004, (available at http://www.worldnetdaily.com/news/archives.asp? AUTHOR_ID=7.)

4) Debra Saunders, "Citizenship troopers," *San Francisco Chronicle*, January 25, 2004.

5) Dinesh D'Souza, *What's So Great About America?*, Regnery Publishing, Inc., 2002.

6) Thomas Sowell, "Utopia vs. the US," Townhall, June 3, 2003 (available at http://www. townhall.com/columnists/thomassowell/ts20030603.shtml.)

7) Oubai Mohammad Shahbandar, "Open Letter from an Arab-American Student," Front Page Magazine June 2, 2003, (available at http://www.frontpagemag.com/Articles/ ReadArticle.asp?ID=8143.)

8) David Limbaugh, "Immigration, part 2: American culture," Townhall, January 13, 2004, (available at http://www.townhall.com/columnists/david limbaugh/ dl20040113.shtml.)

9) Daniel Flynn, *Why the Left Hates America: Exposing the Lies That Have Obscured Our Nation's Greatness*, Three Rivers Press, 2002.

10) Jamie Glazov, "A Conversation with Vladimir Bukovsky," Front Page Magazine May 30, 2003, (available at http://www.frontpagemagazine.com /Articles/Printable. asp?ID=8132.)

11) Suzanne Fields, "No common sense and no love of country," Jewish World Review, June 27, 2002, (available at http://www.jewishworld review.com/cols/fields062702.asp.)

12) Nonie Darwish, "The Daughter of an Arab Warrior Tells Her Tale," Front Page Magazine, December 30, 2002, (available at http://www. frontpagemag.com/Articles/Read Article.asp?ID=5301.)

13) Tatiana Menaker, "Hate America Poetry Class," Front Page Magazine, February 23, 2004, (available at http://www.frontpagemag.com/articles /readarticle.asp?ID=12289&p=1.)

14) Balint Vazsonyi, *America's Thirty Years War*, Regnery Publishing, Inc., 1998.

15) Myles Kantor, "A Cuban Southerner's Defense of the South: An Interview with Dr. Miguel A. Faria, Jr." Lew Rockwell, January 4, 2003, (available at http://www.lewrockwell.com/kantor/kantor77.html.)

16) Jonah Goldberg, "Celebrating America's Independence," Jewish World Review, July 5, 2002, (available at http://www.jewishworldreview. com/cols/jonah070502.asp.)

17) Victor Davis Hanson, *Mexifornia: A State of Becoming*, Encounter Books, 2003.

18) Thomas Sowell, "A new Pearl Harbor," Townhall, September 13, 2001. available at http://www.townhall.com/columnists/thomassowell /ts20010913.shtml.)

19) "War Blog," Front Page Magazine, January 26, 2005, (available at http:// frontpagemag.com/Articles/ReadArticle.asp?ID=16770.)

Egalitarianism Endnotes

1) David Wienir and Marc Bereley, *The Diversity Hoax,* Foundation for Academic Standards & Training, 1999.

2) Paul Greenburg, "The Radical as Conservative," Jewish World Review, January 19, 2004, (available at http://www.jewishworldreview.com/cols/greenberg 11904.asp.)

3) Suzanne Fields, "Segregation In The City," Townhall, May 10, 2001, (available at http://www.townhall.com/columnists/suzannefields/sf20010510.shtml.)

4) Charley Reese, "Mississippi knew its flag was not a race issue," *Orlando Sentinel*, April 19, 2001.

5) B. G. Burkett and Glenna Whitley, *Stolen Valor*, Verity Press, Inc., 1998.

6) Op. Cit., Wiener and Bereley.

7) Ibid.

8) Walter Berns, *Making Patriots*, University of Chicago Press, 2001.

9) Charles J. Sykes, *A Nation of Victims*, St. Martin's Press, New York, NY 1992.

10) Roy Rogers and Dales Evans, *Happy Trails: Our Life Stories*, Simon & Schuster, New York, 1994.

11) Gail Buckley, *American Patriots: The Story of Blacks in the Military from the Revolution to Desert Storm*, Random House, 2001.

12) Op. Cit., Wiener and Bereley.

13) John McWhorter "Toward a Usable Black History," City Journal, Summer, 2001 (available at http://www.city-journal.org/html/11_3_toward_a_usable.html.)

14) Victor Davis Hanson, *Mexifornia: A State of Becoming*, Encounter Books, 2003.

15) Bernard Goldberg, 100 *People Who Are Screwing Up America (and Al Franken is #37)*, Harper Collins Publisher, 2005.

The Right to Vote Endnotes

1) Alan W. Dowd, "No Ordinary Election," Hudson Institute, April 1, 2001, (available at http://www.hudson.org/index.cfm?fuseaction= publication_details&id=1812.)

2) Camille Paglia, "Becoming president under a noxious cloud," Salon, November 15, 2000, (available at http://dir.salon.com/people/col/pagl/ 2000/11/15/recount/index.html.)

3) Dennis Prager, "America the Good," Jewish World Review, April 15, 2003, (available at http://www.jewishworldreview.com/0403/prager 041503.asp.)

The American Flag Endnotes

1) Walter Berns, "From the Ashes, Patriotism Reborn," On the Issues, *American Enterprise*, October 1, 2001.
2) Ronnie Milsap, *Almost Like A Song, McGraw Hill Publishing,* 1990.
3) Julia Gornin, *Patriotism for Dummies*, Jewish World Review, October 1, 2001. (available at http://www.jewishworldreview.com/julia/gorin100101.asp.)
4) Walter Berns, *Making Patriots*, University of Chicago Press, 2001.

Religion Endnotes

1) Doug Giles, "Hacking Away at America's Heritage," Townhall, March 13, 2004, (available at http://www.townhall.com/columnists/douggiles /dg20040313.shtml.)

2) Avery Cardinal Dulles, "John Paul II and the Truth about Freedom," *First Things*, August/September, 1995.

3) "Toward Tradition offers cure for terror anxiety," Toward Tradition press release, November 2, 2001, (available at http://www.towardtradition. org/pr_terroranxiety 11201.htm)

4) Leonard Dinnerstein, *Anti-Semitism in America*, Oxford University Press, 1995.

5) Evelyn Husband with Donna Vanliere, *High Calling*, Thomas Nelson Publishers, Nashville, 2003.

6) Dr. Laura Schlessinger, "The man who should have been governor," World Net Daily, April 6, 2004, (available at http://www.worldnetdaily. com/news/article.asp?ARTICLE_ ID=37901.)

7) Laura Ingraham, *Shut Up and Sing: How Elites from Hollywood, Politics, and the UN are Subverting America*, Regnery Publishing, Inc., 2003.

8) Chaplain Captain Sung-Joo Park, "National Prayer Breakfast to honor military, elected officials, *The Sheppard Senator*, date not provided, (available at http://www.sheppardsenator.com/archives/2005/011405/ a0103.shtml.)

9) William J. Murray, *My Life Without God*, Harvest House Publishers, Inc, 1992.

10) Some sources do not include the word "ravishing."

Thanksgiving Endnotes

1) Dolly Parton, *My Life and Other Unfinished Business*, Harpercollins, 1994.

2) Jesse Lee Peterson, *From Rage to Responsibility*, Continuum International Publishing Group, 2000.

3) Ben Stein, "Fourth is a time of celebration, but also of gratitude," *USA Today*, date not provided, (available at http://www.usatoday.com/news/opinion/editorials/2003-07-02-oplede_x.htm.)

4) Linda Chavez, "National Indulgence Day?," Jewish World Review, November 26, 2003, (available at http://www.jewishworldreview.com/cols/chavez112603.asp.)

5) Armstrong Williams, "Let's remember the heroes this Thanksgiving," Townhall. November 20, 2001, (available at http://www.townhall.com/columnists/Armstrong williams/aw20011120.shtml.)

6) Michelle Malkin, "Thanksgiving Prayer 2002," Townhall, November 27, 2002, (available at http://www.townhall.com/columnists/michelle malkin/mm20021127.shtml.)

7) Hans Zeiger, "The Thankless generation," Men's News Daily, November 23, 2003, available at http://www.mensnewsdaily.com/archive/yz/z-misc/zeiger/03/zeiger 112303.htm.)

BRIEF BIOGRAPHIES OF ALL
QUOTED INDIVIDUALS

A

Abdallah, Ahmed Umar--Islamic cleric

Abdel-Sahib, Ahmed--Iraqi citizen

Abdul, Ibrahim--former Iraqi refugee returning to his liberated homeland

Adams, Abigail--(1744--1818) First Lady to John Adams

Adams, John--(1735--1826) second President of the United States

Adams, John Quincy--(1767--1848) sixth President of the United States

Adams Samuel--(1722--1803) cousin of John Adams and a delegate to the
        Continental Congress

Addison, Joseph--(1672--1719) British author whose play *Cato* was a
        favorite of George Washington

Adkins, Tom--Columnist and commentator

Adler, Felix--(1851--1933) founder of the Ethical Culture movement

Adsit, Jack--World War II veteran and government reform activist

Agha, Mohammed Ismail--former Guantanamo Bay detainee

Aghdashloo, Shohreh--actress, writer, and immigrant from Iran

al-Abid Rabu, Mohammed Tahar--Mosul town council member

al-Gailani, Hadid--gratefully liberated Iraqi citizen

Al-Istrabadi, Feisal Amin--Interim Iraqi Ambassador to the United Nations

Alcott, Louisa May --(1832--1888) author

Allawi, Iyad--Interim Prime Minister of Iraq

Ames, Fisher--(1758--1808) President of Harvard

Anderson, Marian--(1897-1993) opera singer

Anthony, Susan B.--(1820--1906) suffragette and human rights activist

Armey, Dick--former congressman from Texas

Armstrong, Louis--(1901-1971) pioneering jazz musician

Arnett, Peter--disgraced former newscaster

Arthur, Chester A.--(1829--1886) twenty-first President of the United
        States

Ashcroft, John--former Attorney General and former Governor and
        Senator from Missouri

Ayoob, Mohammed--college professor

B

Baadani, Jamal--U.S. Marine and founder of Association of Patriotic Arab Americans in Military

Baldwin, Roger--(1793-1863) abolitionist and attorney

Barber, J. Matt--columnist, boxer, drummer, and attorney

Barton, Clara--(1821--1912) founder of the American Red Cross

Beamer, Todd--(1968--2001) businessman and hero of Flight # 93 on September 11, 2001

Beard, Charles Austin--(1874–1948) American historian and author

Bedawi, Taha--Mayor of Fallujah

Beecher, Henry Ward--(1813--1887) minister, abolitionist, and brother of Harriet Beecher Stowe

Bennett, William--cultural commentator, author, and former Secretary of Education

Bereley, Marc--author and President of the Foundation for Academic Standards & Tradition

Berlin, Irving --(1888--1989) songwriter and immigrant from Russia

Bermudez, Claudia--2004 California congressional candidate, immigrant from Nicaragua, and daughter of Contra Leader Enrique Bermudez

Berns, Walter--historian, college professor, and American Enterprise Institute scholar

Binladin, Abdullah Mohammed--Boston-area resident and Osama Bin Laden's brother

Blackwell, Kenneth--Ohio's Secretary of State and former Treasurer

Blair, Tony--Prime Minister of England

Blum, Ralph--motivational speaker and author

Bodman, Samuel W.--Secretary of Energy and former Deputy Secretary of the Treasury

Boggs, Kelly--columnist for *Baptist Press*

Boone, Daniel--(1735--1820) pioneer and explorer

Bork, Robert--former federal judge, legal analyst, and author

Boudinot, Elias--(1740--1821) New Jersey delegate to and one-time President of the Continental Congress

Boyd, Jr., Ralph F.--Chairman Freddie Mac Foundation and former Assistant Attorney General

Boyd, Susan L.--former law student at Ashbrook University

Bradford, William--(1590--1657) Pilgrim and Governor of Plymouth

Bradley, Omar--(1893--1981) five-star U.S. Army General

Brady, Pat--Vietnam War Army veteran

Brandeis, Louis--(1870--1930) former Supreme Court Justice

Bremer, Paul--former presidential envoy to Iraq and diplomat

Bruce, Tammy--cultural commentator, author, and former head of the Los Angeles Chapter of the National Organization For Women

Buchanan, James--(1791--1868) fifteenth President of the United States

Bukovsky, Vladimir--author and ex-Soviet prisoner of conscience

Bullard, Eugene Jacque--(1894--1961) World War I veteran and the first black citizen to fly a fighter plane

Burke, Edmund--(1729--1797) British statesman, author, and supporter of American Independence

Burkett, B. G.--decorated Vietnam War veteran, author, and exposer of phony Vietnam veterans

Burroughs, William S.--(1914--1997) author and critic

Burt, Jim--U.S. Army veteran and Medal of Honor recipient

Bush, George W.--forty-third President of the United States

Bush, George H.W.--forty-first president of the United States

Byrd, Robert--Senator from West Virginia

C

Cabana, Bob--Johnson Space Center Director of Flight Crew Operations at the time of the tragic Columbia flight

Capra, Frank--(1897--1991) movie director

Carroll, Charles--(1737--1832), signer of the Declaration of Independence and abolitionist

Carroll, John--(1735--1815) the first Catholic bishop in America and the brother of Charles Carroll

Carson, Adam--US Army Captain

Carter, Jimmy--thirty-ninth President of the United States

Carver, George Washington--pioneering agricultural scientist and ex-slave

Chambers, Whittaker--(1901--1961) author and ex-communist

Chapman, Beth--Alabama's State Auditor

Chapman, John Jay--(1862--1933) lawyer, social commentator, and author

Chaput, Charles--Archbishop of Denver

Charen, Mona--columnist and former White House speechwriter

Charlton, Van--(dates unavailable) father of Korean War posthumous Medal of Honor winner Sergeant Cornelius Charlton

Chauncey, Isaac (1779--1840) Unites States Naval Commodore during the War of 1812

Chavez, Linda--President of the Center for Equal Opportunity, author, social commentator, and former Director of the U.S. Commission on Civil Rights

Cheney Dick --George W. Bush's Vice-President and former Secretary of Defense and Congressman from Wyoming

Cheney, Lynn--Wife of Dick Cheney, author, and former Chairman of the National Endowment for the Humanities

Cherry, Fred--Vietnam War fighter pilot who spent over seven years as a prisoner of war

Churchill, Winston--(1874--1965) Prime Minister of England

Cirucci, Adam--reporter and writer

Cleland, Max--former Senator from Georgia

Cleveland, Grover--(1837--1908) twenty-second/twenty-fourth President of the United States

Cohan, George M.--(1878--1942) songwriter and entertainer

Cole, Brian--U.S. Marine Lance Corporal

Cole, Bruce--Chairman of the National Endowment for the Humanities and former college professor

Colfax, Schuyler--(1823--1885) Ulysses S. Grant's Vice-President and Indiana congressman who served as Speaker of the House at the time of Abraham Lincoln's assassination

Colson, Chuck--Watergate figure, author, and founder of Prison Fellowship Ministries

Connolly, D.J.--author and engineer

Coolidge, Calvin--(1872--1933) thirtieth President of the United States

Coulter, Ann--Constitutional attorney, political commentator, and author

Crockett, Davy--(1786--1836) Tennessee Congressman, explorer, and hero of the Alamo

Cronauer, Adrian--Vietnam War Air Force veteran, military disc jockey, and attorney

Curie, Charles--Administrator of the U.S. Department of Health and Human Services' Substance Abuse and Mental Health Services Administration

D

Dale, Helle--syndicated columnist and member of various think tanks

Daniels, Charlie--country singer and musician

Darwish, Nonie--commentator and author on American freedom, founder of Arabs for Israel, and an immigrant from the Middle East who does not reveal her native country for fear of retaliation against relatives still there

Davis, Sr., Benjamin O.--(1897--1970) first Black General in the United States Army

DeMille, Cecil B.--(1881--1959) film director and screenwriter

Dershowitz, Alan--attorney, law professor, commentator, and author

DeVos, Richard--co-founder of Amway

de Tocqueville, Alexis--(1805--1859) French politician, philosopher and admiring observer of America

Diamond, Martin--political scientist, historian, and author

Dickinson, John (1732--1808) statesman and author

Dietrich, Marlene--(1901--1992) actress, singer, and immigrant from Germany

Dinh, Viet--law professor and former Assistant Attorney General credited as the principle author of the Patriot Act

Dinnerstein, Leonard--author and Columbia University Professor Emeritus

Disney, Walt--(1901--1966) entertainment pioneer

Donahue, William--President of the Catholic League for Religious and Civil Liberties

Douglass, Frederick--(1818--1895) abolitionist, orator, and former slave

Douglas, William O.--(1898--1980) Supreme Court Justice

Dowd, Alan W.--columnist and former congressional aide

Driver, William--(1803-1873) ship's captain

D'Souza, Dinesh--author, international expert, and Hoover Institution Fellow

Dulles, Avery --Cardinal in the Catholic Church, college professor, and lecturer

E

Earhart, Amelia--(1897--1937) pioneering aviator

Edison, Thomas--(1847--1931) inventor

Eilert, Richard--author and Vietnam War Marine veteran

Einstein, Albert--(1879--1955) mathematician and intellect

Eisenhower Dwight D.--(1890--1969) thirty-fourth President of the United States

El Yassiri, Ishtar--Iraqi newspaper editor

El-Fadl, Khaled Abou--law professor, Islamic scholar, and author

Emanuelsen, Kathy Lynn--front line nurse during the Vietnam War

Emerson, Ralph Waldo--(1803--1882) poet, author, and philosopher

Evans, Dale--(1912-2001) actress, singer, and humanitarian

F

Fallaci Oriana--journalist, author, and international commentator

Faria, Miguel--physician, author, and former editor of *Medical Sentinel*

Farrah (last name not provided)--Iraqi teenager

Feder, Don--commentator, author, and political consultant

Fields, Suzanne--syndicated columnist

Feinstein, Diane--Senator from California

Fillmore, Millard --(1800-1874) thirteenth President of the United States

Fish, Jr., Hamilton--(1888--1991) Congressman and World War 1 Veteran

Flaih, Salah--convenience store owner, ex-Iraqi army officer, and immigrant

Flynn, Daniel--author and lecturer

Flynn, George Q.--author and retired history professor

Flynt-Vega, Tonya--anti-pornography activist and daughter of infamous pornographer Larry Flynt

Ford, Gerald--thirty-eighth President of the United States

Ford, Henry--(1863--1947) businessman and automobile pioneer

Forrestal, James--(1892--1949) Secretary of Defense

Fosdick, Harry (Henry) Emerson--(1878-1969) minister and author

Frankfurter, Felix--(1882-1965) Supreme Court Justice

Franklin, Benjamin--(1706--1790) inventor, statesman, and diplomat

G

Gadhafi, Seif al-Islam--son of Libya's dictator Muammar Gadhafi

Gantz, Yaffa--author and lecturer

Garfield, James--(1831--1881) twentieth President of the United States

Garrison, William Lloyd--(1805--1879) abolitionist and publisher

Giles, Henry--(1809--1882) minister

Giles, Doug--columnist and radio talk show host

Gilly, Tanya--Democracy Programs Director at the Foundation for the
Defense of Democracies and immigrant from Iraq

Gilmore, James--former Governor of Virginia

Giuliani, Rudolph--Mayor of New York City on September 11, 2001

Godfrey, Arthur--(1903--1983) TV personality, songwriter, and entertainer

Goldberg, Bernard--journalist and author

Goldberg, Jonah--*National Review Online* Editor at Large and syndicated
columnist

Gore, Al--former Vice-President of the United States and 2000
presidential candidate

Gornin, Julia--Columnist and comedienne

Graham, Phillip--(exact dates unknown) colonist and abolitionist

Graham, Billy--minister

Grammer, Kelsey--actor and comedian

Grant, Ulysses S.--(1822--1885) eighteenth President of the United States

Grayson, William--(1740--1790) Virginia delegate to the Continental
Congress

Greeley, Horace--(1811--1872) abolitionist, publisher, and journalist

Greenburg, Paul--Editor of the *Arkansas Democrat-Gazette*

Greene, Nathanael--(1742--1786) Revolutionary War General

Greenspan, Alan--Federal Reserve Board Chairman

H

Hagen, Margaret--psychologist, college professor, and author

Hagee, John--minister, author, and broadcaster

Hagelin, Rebecca--Vice-President of the Heritage Foundation and
columnist

Hamill, Pete--journalist and author

Hamilton, Alexander--(1755--1804) first Secretary of the Treasury and
co-author of *the Federalist Papers*

Hand, Learned--(1872--1961) judge and author

Hanson, Victor Davis--college professor, farmer, and author

Harding, Warren G.--(1865--1920) twenty-ninth President of the United
States

Harlan, John --(1899--1971) Supreme Court Justice

Harris, Dr. (first name and dates unknown)--Revolutionary War veteran
and physician

Harrison, Benjamin--(1833--1901) twenty-third President of the United
States

Harrison, William Henry--(1173--1841) ninth President of the United
States

Hayes, Rutherford B.--(1822-1893) nineteenth President of the United
States

Helms, Jesse--former Senator from North Carolina

Helprin, Mark --novelist and senior fellow at the Claremont Institute

Henderson Jr. Ronald H.--US Navy Captain, commanding officer of *USS
John F. Kennedy*

Henninger, Daniel--editorialist for *the Wall Street Journal*

Henry, O.--(1862--1910) short story writer

Henry, Patrick--(1736--1799) statesman, orator, Governor of
Virginia and Delegate to the Continental Congress

Heston, Charlton--actor and civil rights activist

Heston, Lydia--Charlton Heston's wife of over 60 years

Himmelfarb, Gertrude--scholar, author, and commentator

Hollowell, Kelly--columnist, attorney, and founder of Science Ministries

Holmes, Oliver Wendell--(1841--1935) Supreme Court Justice

Holton, Paul--Army National Guardsman and humanitarian

Hoover, Herbert--(1874--1964) thirty-first President of the United States

Hope, Bob--(1903--2003) comedian, actor, and humanitarian

Hopkins, Stephen--(1707--1785) Declaration of Independence signer from Massachusetts

Howard, John--Prime Minister of Australia

Huckabee, Mike--Governor of Arkansas and author

Hughes, Charles Evans--(1862--1948) Supreme Court Justice and Secretary of State

Humphrey, Hubert--(1911--1978) Lyndon Johnson's Vice-President

Husband, Rick--astronaut and United States Air Force veteran

I

Ibrahim (last name not provided)--Iraqi citizen

Ingersoll, Robert Green--(1833-1899), Civil War veteran, orator, statesman, and civil rights activist

Ingraham, Laura--talk show host, author, and attorney

J

Jackson, Thomas J.--(1824--1863) Confederate General

Jackson, Andrew--(1767--1845) seventh President of the United States

Jackson, Alphonso--Secretary of Housing and Urban Development

Jackson, Robert H.--(1892--1954) Supreme Court Justice and Nuremberg prosecutor

Jacobs, Joanne--education reformer and columnist

Jacoby, Jeff--syndicated columnist

Jasser, M. Zuhdi--Chairman of the Islamic Forum for Democracy, physician, and Navy veteran

Jay, John --(1745--1829) first Chief Justice of the United States Supreme Court, statesman, and abolitionist

Jefferson, Thomas--(1743--1826) third President of the United States

John Paul II--(1920--1985) Pope

Johnson, Andrew (1708--1875) seventeenth President of the United States

Johnson, Lyndon (1908--1973) thirty-sixth President of the United States

Jordan, Barbara (1936--1996) Texas Congresswoman

Josephson, Michael--ethicist and commentator

Joyce, Russell--US Army Special Forces Sergeant First Class
Justis, Marty--Executive Director of Citizens Flag Alliance

K

Kabbani, Muhammad Hisham --Muslim cleric and Chairman of the
    Islamic Supreme Council of America
Kane, Gregory--columnist for *the Baltimore Sun*
Kashi, Rania --Iraqi expatriate
Kathuria, Chirinjeev--physician, politician, and immigrant from India
Kazim, Yusuf Abed--Iraqi citizen
Keller, Helen (1880--1968) author and inspiring example
Kennedy, John (1917--1963) thirty-fifth President of the United States
Kennedy, Robert (1925--1968) Attorney General
Kerry, John--senator from Massachusetts and 2004 presidential candidate
Kim, Marshall--businessman and immigrant from Cambodia
King, Jr., Martin Luther--(1929--1968) minister and civil rights activist
King, Rufus--(1755--1827) statesman and diplomat
Kishtaini, Khalid--Iraqi author
Kissinger, Henry--former Secretary of State and statesman
Koch, Ed--former Mayor of New York City, author, and columnist
Krauthammer, Charles--columnist and former physician

L

Lai, Madalenna--Freedom activist and immigrant from Vietnam
Lapin, Daniel--rabbi, author, lecturer, and Founder and President of
    Toward Tradition
Lasorda, Tommy--former major league baseball manager
Lazarus, Emma--(1849--1887) poet and author
Lee, Robert E.--(1807--1870) Confederate General
Lee, Brenda--singer and entertainer
Leno, Jay--comedian and host of *The Tonight Show*
Lewis, Sinclair --(1885-1951) author
Lieberman, Joseph--Senator from Connecticut
Limbaugh, David--attorney and syndicated columnist
Lincoln, Abraham --(1809--1865) sixteenth President of the United States

Lippman, Walter (1889--1974) statesman and author

Lo, Chaxiong--community activist and immigrant from Laos

Lodge, Henry Cabot--(1850--1924) Senator and Congressman from
    Massachusetts

Luce, Clare Booth--(1903--1987) diplomat, editor, and playwright

M

Mahdi, M.--Former Iraqi Republican Guardsman

MacArthur, Douglas--(1880-1964) Five-Star US Army General

Madison, James--(1751--1836) fourth President of the United States

Malkin, Michelle--syndicated columnist and author

Mandrell, Barbara--country singer and actress

Mamoud, Raad--former Iraqi soldier

Marshall John--(1755-1835) Supreme Court Chief Justice

Marshall, Thurgood--(1908--1993) Supreme Court Justice

Martinez, Mel--Senator from Florida and former Secretary of Housing and
    Urban Development

Masry, Omar--Army Sergeant and blogger

Mayer, Tim--2nd Lieutenant stationed in Iraq

McCain, John--Senator from Arizona

McCormick, Heather--former law student at Berkeley

McDonald, Stephen--Decorated New York City Police Officer and
    humanitarian

McCullough, David--American historian and author

McGovern, George--former Senator from South Dakota, statesman, and
    1972 presidential candidate

McKinley, William--(1843--1901) twenty-fourth President of the United
    States

McMillian, Craige--columnist, publisher, and talk show host

McWhorter John--linguist, author, college professor, commentator, and
    Manhattan Institute Fellow

Meese, Edwin--former Attorney General

Medved, Michael--columnist, movie reviewer, and radio talk show host

Melville, Herman--(1819--1891) author

Menaker, Tatiana--student activist, former journalist, and immigrant from
    the Soviet Union
Mencken, H.L.--journalist, editor, and critic
Miller, Dennis--comedian, commentator, and talk show host
Miller, Zell--former Governor and Senator from Georgia
Milsap, Ronnie--country singer
Mohammed, Faiz--former Guantanamo Bay detainee
Mohammed, Marlon--actor and commentator
Monroe, James--(1758--1831) fifth President of the United States
Moore, Roy--former Alabama Supreme Court Chief Justice
Morris, Lewis--(1726--1798) New Jersey Governor and New York State
    Supreme Court Justice
Moynihan, Daniel Patrick--(1927--2003) Senator from New York,
    statesman, and cultural commentator
Munson, Lynne--former Deputy Chairman of the National Endowment for
    the Humanities, author, and cultural critic
Murray, William J.--Chairman of the Religious Freedom Coalition, and
    son of infamous atheist Madalyn Murray O'Hare
Mutia, Ofelia Bayutas --blogger and human rights activist

N
Nathan, George Jean--(1882–1958) editor and critic
Netanyahu, Binyamin--former Prime Minister of Israel
Nimitz, Chester W.--(1885--1966) US Navy Admiral
Nixon, Richard--(1913-1994) thirty-seventh President of the United States
Noonan, Peggy--columnist, author, and former White House speechwriter
North, Mike--columnist and land surveyor
Norton, Gale--Secretary of the Interior and former Colorado State
    Attorney General

O
Obama, Barack--Senator from Illinois
O'Keefe, Georgia--(1887--1946) painter
Olson, Barbara--(1955--2001) attorney, author, commentator, and victim
    of the September 11 attacks

O'Malley, Sean P.--Bishop of the Boston Archdiocese
O'Neal, John--Vietnam War Navy Veteran, attorney, and author

P

Page, William Tyler--(1868--1942) former Clerk of the US House of
    Representatives
Paige, Rod--former Secretary of Education and school reform advocate
Paglia, Camille--author, cultural commentator, and college professor
Pahlavi, Reza--son of the last Shah of Iraq
Paine Thomas--(1737--1809) author, editor, and publisher
Park, Sung-Joo--captain/chaplain in the United States Air Force
Parker, Kathleen--syndicated columnist and educator
Parker, Richard--legal scholar
Parks, David--Vietnam War Army Veteran
Parton, Dolly--country singer, actress, and businesswoman
Pataki, George--Governor of New York on September 11, 2001
Patton, George S.--(1885--1945) US Army General
Pell, Claiborne--former Senator from Rhode Island
Penn, William--(1644--1718) proprietor of Pennsylvania, author, and
    religious freedom advocate
Perle, Richard--Pentagon advisor and former Undersecretary of Defense
Perry, John L.--columnist and editor
Petersen, Jesse Lee--community activist and founder of Brotherhood
    Organization of a New Destiny (BOND)
Pickford, Mary--(1893--1979) actress and immigrant from Canada
Pierce, Franklin--(1804--1869) fourteenth President of the United States
Podhoretz, Norman--author, columnist, and former editor of *Commentary*
Polk, James--(1795-1849) eleventh President of the United States
Ponte, Lowell--columnist, editor, and radio talk show host
Potasnik, Joseph--rabbi and talk show host
Powell, Colin--former Secretary of State and former Chairman of the Joint
    Chiefs of Staff
Prager, Dennis--author, commentator, and radio talk show host
Presser, Stephen B.--law professor and historian

Q

Quinn, Isabelle --former law student at Berkeley

R

Radosh, Ronald--author, commentator, and former communist

Rahim, Ayad--journalist and immigrant from Iraq

Rayburn, Sam--(1882--1961) Speaker of the House

Ronald Reagan--(1911--2004) fortieth President of the United States

Reese, Charley--columnist

Rell, Jodi--Governor of Connecticut

Reynolds, Gerald--Chairman of the US Commission on Civil Rights, and former Deputy Associate Attorney General

Rice, Condoleezza--Secretary of State and former National Security Advisor

Rivers, Joan--comedian, author, and talk show host

Riddle, Wesley Allen--historian and author

Roberts, Paul Craig--author, columnist and member of various think tanks

Rodriguez, Gregory--author and commentator

Rogers, Will--(1879–1935) commentator and entertainer

Roosevelt, Franklin Delano--(1882--1945) thirty-second President of the United States

Roosevelt, Eleanor--(1884--1962) First Lady to Franklin Delano Roosevelt

Roosevelt, Theodore--(1858-1919) twenty-sixth President of the United States

Root, Elihu--(1845--1937) Secretary of State, Secretary of Defense, and Senator from New York

Rumsfeld, Donald--Secretary of Defense

Rush, Benjamin (1745--1813) physician, chemist, abolitionist, and Pennsylvania delegate to the Continental Congress

Rutter, Scott E.--military analyst and Desert Storm army veteran

S

Sabrin, Murray--college professor and commentator

Safer, Morley--broadcast journalist

Saga, Sarah--American citizen held prisoner in Saudi Arabia by her Saudi father for over 16 years before her release

Salih, Barham--Iraqi statesman

Sandburg, Carl--(1878--1967) poet and author

Sarton, May--(1912--1995) poet and immigrant from Belgium

Saunders, Debra--syndicated columnist

Scalia, Antonin--Supreme Court Justice

Schippers, David--congressional attorney during impeachment and author

Schlesinger, Jr., Arthur--statesman and author

Schlessinger, Laura--radio talk show host, author, and physiologist

Schramm, Peter--scholar, college professor, and former Education Department official

Schundler, Bret--former Mayor of Jersey City

Schwarzkopf, Norman--former US Army General

Shabazz, Ak'Bar--commentator and businessman

Shahbandar, Oubai Mohammad--former student activist at Arizona State University and immigrant from Syria

Shamsid-Dean, Elbert--American Muslim

Shapiro, Alexander M.--(birth year unavailable--1992) rabbi and one-time Rabbinical Assembly President

Shapiro, Ben--columnist, author, and law student

Shawcross, William--British journalist

Shirer, William--(1904--1993) historian, journalist, and author

Simpson, Barbara--columnist and talk show host

Skelton, Red--(1913-1997) entertainer and humanitarian

Smirnoff, Yakov--comedian, businessman, and immigrant from the Soviet Union

Smith, William---attorney

Snow, Tony--talk show host and commentator

Sowell, Thomas--economist, author, and columnist

St. Jean de Crevecoeur, Hector--(1735--1813) colonial farmer and author

Stein, Ben--comedian, actor, commentator, author, and attorney

Stevens, John Paul--Supreme Court Justice

Stevenson, Adlai--(1900--1965) Governor of Illinois and two-time presidential candidate

Steward, Theophilus G.--(1843--1924) Army chaplain
Steyn, Mark--columnist, critic, and Canadian citizen
Story, Joseph--(1779-1845) Supreme Court Justice
Stowe, Harriet Beecher--(1811--1896) author and abolitionist
Stratton, Lawrence M.--attorney and author
Strickland, Eric L.--computer programmer
Sunday, Billy--(1862--1935) minister
Sutherland, George--(1862--19432) Supreme Court Justice
Sykes, Charles J.--author and education reform advocate

T

Taft, William Howard--(1857--1930) twenty-seventh President of the
   United States
Taheri, Amir--Iranian expatriate, journalist, and commentator
Taranto, James--columnist for *the Wall Street Journal*
Taylor, Zachary--(1784--1850) twelfth President of the United States
Terrell, Suzanne--former Louisiana Elections Commissioner
Thibault, David--reporter
Thomas, Cal--author and columnist
Thoreau, Henry David--(1817--1862) author and philosopher
Tiner, Stan--executive editor of the *Sun Herald*
Truman, Harry S.--(1884-1972) thirty-third President of the United States
Truth, Sojourner--(1797--1883) ex-slave, suffragette, abolitionist, and
   lecturer
Tubman, Harriet--(1820--1913) ex-slave and abolitionist
Twain, Mark--(1835--1910) author
Tyler, John (1790--1862) tenth President of the United States

U

Usman, Azhar--comedian, lecturer, and attorney

V

Van Buren, Martin--(1782--7862) eighth President of the United States
Vaughan, Bill--(1915--1977) columnist and author

Vazsonyi, Balint--(1936--2003) Founder and President of the Center of the American Founding, author, commentator, and concert pianist

Velasquez, Jose--immigrant from El Salvador

von Braun, Wernher (1912--1977) space exploration advocate

W

Ward, Christopher--Vietnam-era Naval Veteran and former reporter

Warren, Earl--(1891--1974) Supreme Court Chief Justice

Warren, Joseph--(1740--1775) statesman and Revolutionary War veteran

Washington, Booker T.--(1856-1915) author, orator, founder of the Tuskegee Institute, and ex-slave

Washington, George--(1732--1799) first President of the United States

Wayne, John--(1907--1979) actor

Weaver, C. Mason--author and speaker

Webster, Daniel--(1782--1852) statesman, orator, and attorney

Webster, Noah--(1758--1843) dictionary compiler, editor, publisher, educator, and school reform advocate

Weinberg, Noah--rabbi and author

Wheeler, Daniel S.--President of Citizens Flag Alliance

White, Theodore--(1915--1986) historian, journalist, and novelist

Whitman, Walt--(1819--1892) poet, journalist, and essayist

Wienir, David--attorney and author

Wilkie, Wendell--(1892-1944) businessman and 1940 presidential candidate

Will, George--columnist and author

Williams, Armstrong --talk show host and columnist

Williamson, Richard S.--former Alternate Representative for Special Political Affairs to the United Nations

Wilson, James--(1742-1798) statesman and Declaration of Independence signer

Wilson, Woodrow--(1856--1924) twenty-eighth President of the United States

Winthrop, Robert C.-- (1809--1894) Senator and Congressman from Massachusetts

Wolfe, Thomas--(1900--1938) author
Woods, Tiger--golfer

Y

Yeagley, David--columnist and blogger
Yahia, Latif--former double for Uday Hussein
Yu, Eugene Chin--businessman and veteran affairs activist

Z

Zebari, Hoshyar--Interim Iraqi Minister of Foreign Affairs
Ziegler, Hans--columnist, author, and founder of Scout Honor Coalition
Ziglar, Zig--motivational speaker
Zinsmeister, Karl--editor of *American Enterprise* and author

Amazingly after 13 chapters paying tribute to the best of America, so much remains unsaid. No topic here received more than the most cursory coverage, and many important subjects were not even broached. For a country like the United States of America where endless opportunities abound, there is no limit to the quotes that could be used in a work of this nature. In the short time between sending this work to press and its publication, I came across a plethora of additional quotes that I wish could have been included. Fortunately, it does not take a psychic to predict that many similar books will be written in the future, and untold patriotic statements will be stirringly expressed by tomorrow's grateful Americans. While *Of Thee I Speak* is far from comprehensive, it puts forth a heartfelt effort to say "Thank You" to the greatest country on God's green earth.

Hopefully, the contents of this book helped imbue your patriotism, but these impressive words are meaningless without proper actions behind them. Perhaps the book's most salient contribution would be in serving as an impetus for even a few readers to take concrete steps to help make the United States an even better country. Endless volunteer opportunities are readily available all across America. Unsung American heroes labor around the clock in alcohol and drug rehabilitation centers, homeless shelters, at veterans' facilities, nursing homes, and in numerous other institutions, assisting their less fortunate fellow citizens. By helping military families cope, comforting crime victims, mentoring youths whose lives have gone awry, and performing endless other good deeds, they directly benefit a few fellow citizens and collectively make America's star shine brighter. If it acts as a catalyst for even one person to become a more grateful, respectful, proud, active American, then *Of Thee I Speak* will have loudly enunciated an important message.

Steven Fantina is the webmaster/editor of Word of the Day (www.wordofthedaywebsite.com.) He is a lifelong resident of New Jersey and very thankful to be living in the greatest country on earth.

He is also the author of *101 Words You'll Probably Never Need To Know But Can Use To Impress People* available through Integritous Press. He can be reached at webmaster@wordofthedaywebsite.com.